Cambridge Elements

Elements in Business Strategy
edited by
J.-C. Spender
Kozminski University

THE DEMISE OF THE GLOBAL ICE INDUSTRY

China's Stunning Role in Leading the BEV Revolution

Arie Lewin
Duke University, Fuqua School of Business

Martin Kenney
University of California, Davis - Human Ecology and Co-Director Berkeley Roundtable on the International Economy

El (Emily) Shu
North China University of Technology

Liang Mei
Peking University, National School of Development

Shaftesbury Road, Cambridge CB2 8EA, United Kingdom

One Liberty Plaza, 20th Floor, New York, NY 10006, USA

477 Williamstown Road, Port Melbourne, VIC 3207, Australia

314–321, 3rd Floor, Plot 3, Splendor Forum, Jasola District Centre, New Delhi – 110025, India

103 Penang Road, #05–06/07, Visioncrest Commercial, Singapore 238467

Cambridge University Press is part of Cambridge University Press & Assessment, a department of the University of Cambridge.

We share the University's mission to contribute to society through the pursuit of education, learning and research at the highest international levels of excellence.

www.cambridge.org
Information on this title: www.cambridge.org/9781009455398
DOI: 10.1017/9781009455435

© Arie Lewin, Martin Kenney, El (Emily) Shu and Liang Mei 2025

This publication is in copyright. Subject to statutory exception and to the provisions of relevant collective licensing agreements, with the exception of the Creative Commons version the link for which is provided below, no reproduction of any part may take place without the written permission of Cambridge University Press & Assessment.

An online version of this work is published at doi.org/10.1017/9781009455435 under a Creative Commons Open Access license CC-BY-NC 4.0 which permits re-use, distribution and reproduction in any medium for non-commercial purposes providing appropriate credit to the original work is given and any changes made are indicated. To view a copy of this license visit https://creativecommons.org/licenses/by-nc/4.0

When citing this work, please include a reference to the DOI 10.1017/9781009455435

First published 2025

A catalogue record for this publication is available from the British Library

ISBN 978-1-009-45539-8 Hardback
ISBN 978-1-009-45541-1 Paperback
ISSN 2515-0693 (online)
ISSN 2515-0685 (print)

Additional resources for this publication at www.cambridge.org/lewin.

Cambridge University Press & Assessment has no responsibility for the persistence or accuracy of URLs for external or third-party internet websites referred to in this publication and does not guarantee that any content on such websites is, or will remain, accurate or appropriate.

For EU product safety concerns, contact us at Calle de José Abascal, 56, 1°, 28003 Madrid, Spain, or email eugpsr@cambridge.org

The Demise of the Global ICE Industry

China's Stunning Role in Leading the BEV Revolution

Elements in Business Strategy

DOI: 10.1017/9781009455435
First published online: September 2025

Arie Lewin
Duke University, Fuqua School of Business

Martin Kenney
University of California, Davis - Human Ecology and Co-Director Berkeley Roundtable on the International Economy

El (Emily) Shu
North China University of Technology

Liang Mei
Peking University, National School of Development

Author for correspondence: Arie Lewin, ayl3@duke.edu

Abstract: The precipitous growth of the EV industry in China and its rise to global leadership are astounding and could not have been predicted a decade ago. This growth was propelled by Chinese central government initiatives embedded in several five-year plans that directed attention to a vaguely defined idea of "new energy" vehicles (NEVs). Bottom-up responses to these initiatives involved many new entrepreneurial startups, intense interprovincial competition, and local government support for NEVs. The surge of entrepreneurial startups enabled China to lead in production and technological innovation in this developing EV industry and led to the disruption of the internal combustion engine industry. The Element is an in depth study of how China emerged to dominate the global EV industry and to batteries becoming the most important arena of global technological competition in the early twenty-first century. This title is also available as Open Access on Cambridge Core.

This Element also has a video abstract:
www.cambridge.org/EBUS_Lewin_abstract

Keywords: Tesla, electric vehicles, global automotive industry, disruption of ICE industry, electric batteries

© Arie Lewin, Martin Kenney, El (Emily) Shu and Liang Mei 2025

ISBNs: 9781009455398 (HB), 9781009455411 (PB), 9781009455435 (OC)
ISSNs: 2515-0693 (online), 2515-0685 (print)

Contents

1 Introduction — 1

2 The Early History of Battery-Powered Cars — 11

3 The Rise of the Chinese EV Industry — 15

4 Emergence of the EV Supplier Ecosystem in China — 36

5 Globalization of the Chinese EV Industry — 47

6 Conclusion: The Transformation of the Global Automotive Industry — 52

References — 61

1 Introduction

In architectural technological revolutions, new entrants often disrupt and even undermine and displace incumbent firms whose competitive advantages are based on the existing technological paradigm. The internal combustion engine (ICE) industry, which is based on hydrocarbons and emerged 150 years ago, faces such a disruption, driven by global warming and political and government policies that target decarbonization as well as by market forces that drive the replacement of ICE vehicles with battery-powered electric vehicles (EVs). This disruption is expected to make past capital investment in infrastructure in the ICE industry and the technological knowledge that underpins the business models of ICE producers obsolete.[1]

The contemporary EV industry was initiated by Tesla, the Silicon Valley–based entrant founded in 2003, which produced its millionth car on March 9, 2020. By the end of 2021, it had become the world's largest producer of EVs, only to be surpassed in 2024 by BYD, a Chinese manufacturer. BYD, a startup, began as a manufacturer of rechargeable batteries and expanded to auto manufacturing in 2003, and by 2024 it became the world's largest producer of EVs. The EV technological revolution is driving a momentous geopolitical shift, as China is on track to becoming the EV technological leader. This is facilitated by its emergence as the dominant manufacturer of EVs and their components and the largest market for EVs. This is important as well for most related components – in particular, the batteries, and the increasingly intense competition in drivetrain components that power these vehicles[2] – and in combination with its leadership in the production of renewable energy equipment.

The motivation for this Element was an issue of the *Management and Organization Review* Forum on Tesla in 2018 that initiated a debate whether or not China could reshape the global auto industry and attracted wide attention in the academic and wider community (Teece 2018). Teece (2018) applied the dynamic capability framework (Teece et al. 1997) to review the growth of the Chinese auto industry and concluded that the China-based ICE joint ventures would not build parallel EV capabilities there. Although doing so was technically feasible, these firms would not chose do so because they would not want to

---

[1] In this Element, "electrical vehicles" means automobiles. However, this transition will affect all kinds of vehicles, including trucks, buses, construction equipment, motorcycles, lawn mowers, and others, such as e-scooters and e-bicycles. Concomitant with this transition is a negative feedback loop with the likely deterioration of the entire fossil fuel energy complex. More concretely, a lower number of consumers of gasoline will lead to a lower number of gas stations, and fewer mechanics qualified to work on ICE vehicles. Thus, it will become more expensive to operate an ICE vehicle – a dynamic that could become self-reinforcing.

[2] Foreign firms, such as Bosch, Aisin, and Magna, remain competitive in electric motors and have major operations in China, including R&D.

compete with their highly profitable domestic ICE market. Agreeing with MacDuffie (2018), Teece argued that Tesla would find it challenging to build up the EV supply ecosystem manufacturing capability of a large-scale EV manufacturer in the United States, though, at that time unobserved, China was in the process of building an entire EV supply chain ecosystem from mineral mining to end-of-life recycling (in contrast, five years later, see Jiang and Lu 2023).

In 2018, the perspective advanced by Teece and MacDuffie may have been on target, given the contexts, capabilities, and embedded "lock in" of ICE's technology and mindset, which had been framed by the earlier EV developments initiated by ICE producers. Overcoming the century-old path-dependent trajectory developed by the ICE-powered automotive ecosystem meant that creating a new trajectory and ecosystem appeared to be an exceedingly difficult challenge (Kanger et al. 2019). This difficulty is demonstrated by the fate of the early mass-produced all-EVs, such as the GM EV1, which was abandoned in 2002 despite a relatively positive market reaction. Lead-acid battery–powered EVs were mostly confined to specialized uses, such as golf carts, forklifts, and government-subsidized niches. However, this was about to change, as battery technology advanced initially with the Toyota Prius cobalt-based batteries and when the Silicon Valley startup Tesla became the most important newcomer in the US auto industry since 1947; under its iconic owner, Elon Musk, Tesla eventually became the world's leading EV manufacturer until being displaced by BYD in 2024 (Perkins & Murmann 2018).[3] This transition would be accelerated by the supersession of cobalt-based batteries by lithium iron phosphate (LFP) and, perhaps, eventually sodium – in both of which Chinese firms are leaders.

Despite Tesla's remarkable success, the center of global technological, market, and manufacturing leadership in EVs rapidly shifted to China, even as management scholars hotly debated the strategic and organizational inertia of ICE automakers and industry (Murmann & Vogt 2023). This shift soon led Tesla to find it strategically necessary to build what became its largest factory in Shanghai both to actively compete in the Chinese market and export globally. The shift to China has resulted in automotive history being written at "the speed of China." For example, only ten months passed between Tesla's completion of an agreement with the Shanghai government for the construction of its Gigafactory and the commencement of production.

---

[3] Before Tesla Motors, the last US-listed automaker was the Tucker Corporation, which had its initial public offering in 1947 and went bankrupt in 1950. Although European and Japanese imports subsequently eroded the market share of the "Big Three," no other US firm entered the mass production of automobiles prior to Tesla.

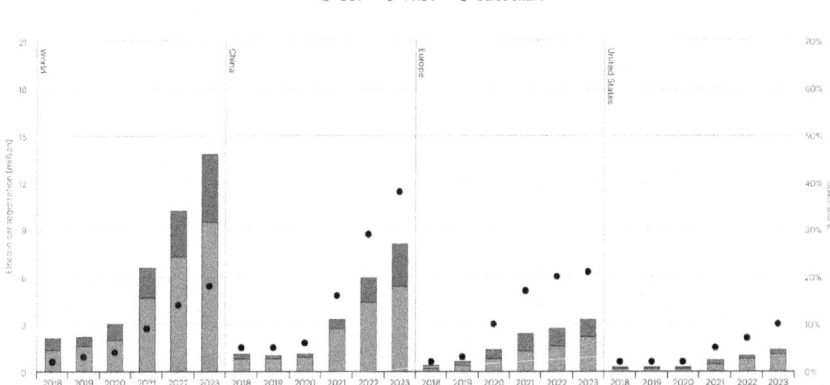

Figure 1 Electric car registration and sales share in China, the United States, and Europe, 2018–2023

Source: IEA, 2024, www.iea.org/reports/global-ev-outlook-2024/trends-in-electric-cars/.

To understand the importance of the Chinese EV market, we need to comprehend its size and its growth rate. Figure 1 summarizes the annual sales volume of EVs from 2018 to 2023.

The growth in China continued apace as in January 2025, 790,842 EVs were sold, and increase of 21 percent year on year (*AutoVista* 2025a). This exceeded the goal of the central government for sales of new energy vehicles (NEVs) to capture 20 percent of the market for cars in the country by 2025 (MIIT 2017). In contrast, in 2024, nearly 1.3 million EVs were sold in the United States (mostly Teslas) (Cox Automotive 2025), and nearly 2.96 million produced by Tesla and, in particular, legacy German automakers were sold in Europe (*AutoVista* 2025b). In other words, more EVs were sold in China than in Europe and the United States combined (O'Donovan 2024).

As Figure 2 indicates, among the top-twenty global OEM groups in terms of EV sales in the first half of 2024, ten were Chinese. BYD sold nearly 1.6 million vehicles (EV and PHEV), making it in the top spot worldwide. Meanwhile, sales of its biggest rival, Tesla, fell by nearly 7 percent over the previous year, relegating it to second place – though admittedly market-share leadership may still fluctuate between BYD and Tesla due to various economic factors, including uncertainty in global trade. Perhaps more important, batteries are the highest value-added component in EVs, and, since 2018, Chinese battery manufacturers have steadily increased their market share to become global leaders, surpassing the previous leaders in South Korea and Japan. In fact, the entire EV value chain

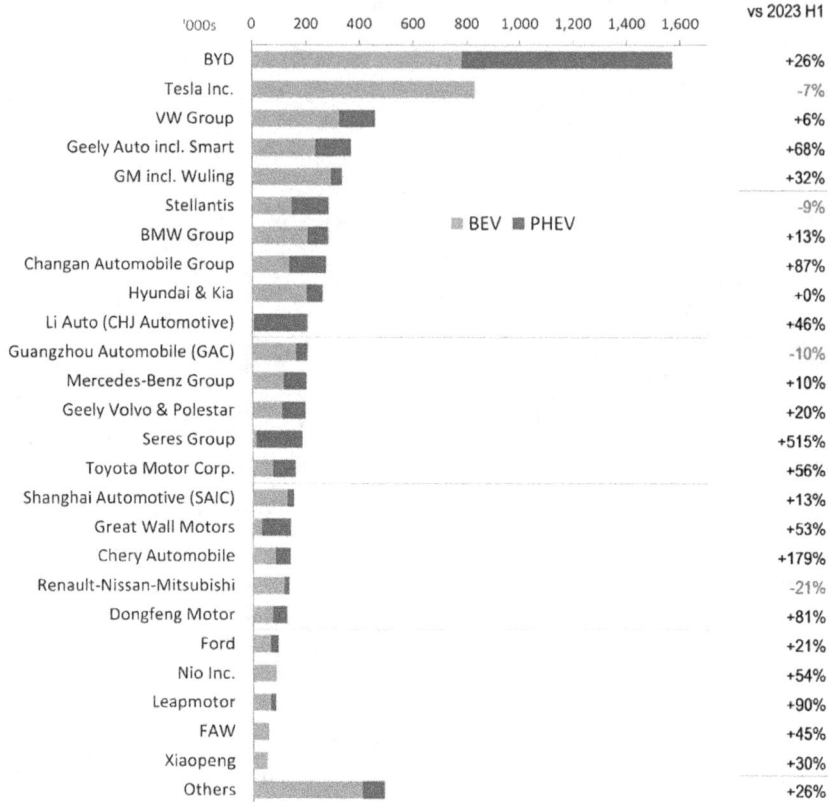

Figure 2 Global EV sales by OEM groups in the first half of 2024
Source: EV Volumes-Aggregated BEV & PHEV sales by model and country

is experiencing a similar shift to Chinese leadership, led by rapid growth in the huge domestic market.

As shown in Figure 3, at the beginning of 2024, the two largest EV battery producers were Contemporary Amperex Technology Co., Limited (CATL), and BYD. These two companies accounted for 55.1 percent of the global market, and when other smaller Chinese battery manufacturers (CALB, Gotion, Sunwoda, and Eve) are included, the Chinese share increases to 67.1 percent. It is noteworthy that no US firms are among the leaders, and the market share of Chinese battery producers has seemingly inexorably increased.

In general, if competing ICE technologies are inexpensive, EVs would not be the runaway success that the Chinese government expects. The early efforts and failures of EVs suggest that "crossing the chasm" (Moore 2014) required EVs to become economically competitive, considering that a car is the most expensive consumer durable purchased. In contrast to the major Western ICE brands, and

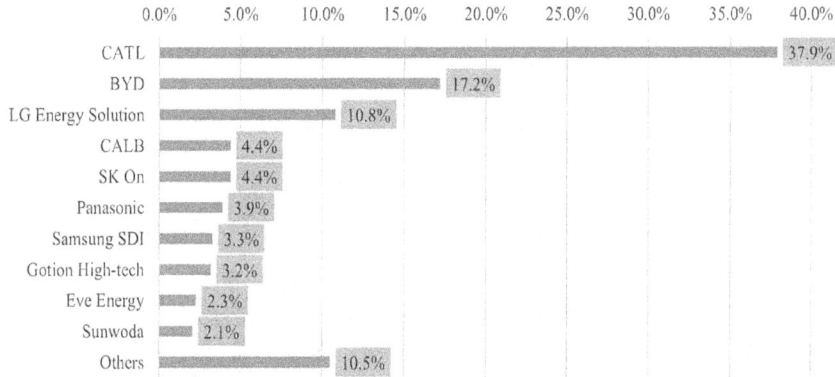

Figure 3 Market share of world's top EV battery manufacturers (January–December 2024)

Source: https://cnevpost.com/2025/02/11/global-ev-battery-market-share-2024/.
Note: CATL, BYD, CALB, Gotion, Sunwoda, and Eve are Chinese; LG, SK, and Samsung are Korean; and Panasonic is Japanese.

even Tesla, Chinese companies increased the economic competitiveness of electric cars by moving them from a niche luxury to the mass market through technological advances in batteries, production efficiency, and massive capacity to capture economies of scale, all of which resulted in an ongoing ferocious price war that drives dramatic price decreases.

This was illustrated in July 2020, when the SAIC-GM-Wuling joint venture introduced the Wuling Hongguang (WH) Mini EV, a fully roadworthy EV, priced from $4,162 to $5,607, depending on the model – making it a car that most Chinese families and, indeed, buyers globally could afford. In less than two months after its debut, the WH Mini EV surpassed Tesla's Model 3 in the top spot for China domestic sales, sparking a boom in ultracompact EVs after it was given the nickname of being the "god car."

The success of the WH Mini EV demonstrates enormous demand for smaller, more affordable EVs, and Chinese manufacturers are well placed to satisfy this demand. Not surprisingly, other domestic manufacturers quickly entered the ever-expanding market for low-cost, light vehicles by launching competing models. The first contender, Chery Automobile, a long-established manufacturer, launched the QQ Ice Cream at the end of 2021; this vehicle was similar to the WH Mini EV in appearance and performance but had an even lower price. The leading state-owned automaker, Chang'an Automobile, also joined the price war by launching the Lumin, an ultracompact EV, in June 2022. In addition, Geely Automobile launched the Panda Mini, targeting female consumers. In 2023, the escalating price war eventually sparked price decreases by

BYD, which launched the Seagull, its least-expensive EV, with a price of $9,700 and a competitive advantage based on its cutting-edge blade batteries and e-platform 3.0 system.

Although, at this point, BYD is unlikely to introduce the Seagull EV in the US market, it is already available in Brazil, at a starting list price of $20,000, far less than for any models offered by Tesla. The existing ICE joint ventures are finding that their survival in the Chinese market is increasingly threatened by sharp price competition from local EV manufacturers.

This is accompanied by the reality that, after facing years of fierce competition in the Chinese domestic market, coupled with the sunsetting of various central government subsidies, hundreds of smaller Chinese EV manufacturers and brands are being driven out of the market as it consolidates. The December 5, 2023, issue of the Japanese magazine *Economist Weekly* reported that about 96 EV manufacturers had a record of production, only 41 of which had an annual production capacity of more than 10,000 vehicles. Ten manufacturers accounted for 70 percent of the Chinese domestic market, and eleven of the twenty top-selling brands in China were domestic. According to a Bloomberg analysis of data from the China Automotive Technology Research Center (CATARC), in July 2023, Chinese domestic automakers, led by BYD and Geely Automobile, accounted for 50 percent of domestic market sales for the first time, having taken a portion of the market share from state-owned–foreign joint ventures producing ICE autos. This suggests that the automotive market in China will experience a shakeout among the smaller EV and ICE producers – many of which are foreign–Chinese joint ventures.[4] Only Tesla has been able to withstand this onslaught of price cutting.[5] In many respects, the current developments in the EV industry in China echo what happened earlier in the US personal computer industry and the early days of the US ICE industry: a massive number of entrants, wild experimentation, an acceleration in technological change followed by a massive shakeout (e.g., Utterback and Suárez 1993).

Because China has established itself as the leading market and manufacturer, in 2024 foreign firms were compelled to invest there in order to secure access to local EV technologies and markets. This was the opposite of the rationale for their ICE investments, which involved technology transfers of outdated foreign

---

[4] For example, Hyundai Motor Company put its production facilities in China up for sale (January 17, 2024), and Stellantis closed its Jeep plant in China in 2022. VW lost its status as China's top-selling car brand to BYD, and even Mercedes-Benz is facing fierce price competition in the Chinese market. Further, previous market leaders in China, such as Toyota, are experiencing waning demand for their ICE and hybrid vehicles.

[5] https://worldpopulationreview.com/country-rankings/tesla-sales-by-country/.

technology to their Chinese partners (Chu 2011). This reversal is exemplified by a decision by VW in July 2023 to invest $700 million to acquire a 5 percent stake in the EV manufacturer Xpeng Automobile, in an effort to boost its position in the Chinese market. VW also made large investments, including acquisition of a majority stake in its joint venture with JAC Motors focused on the production of small EVs and the establishment of an R&D center in Hefei, in Anhui Province. Other investment activities by German legacy manufacturers include Daimler-Benz's investment in the production of small EVs by BAIC and the opening of an R&D center in Beijing. After the Chinese government lifted restrictions on the ratio of capital contribution at foreign joint ventures (JVs), BMW announced plans to increase its stake in its Chinese joint ventures from 50 percent to 75 percent. There is growing recognition that the paradigm shift toward electrification creates new opportunities for Chinese automakers to compete overseas and foreign firms to export EVs made by their Chinese JVs.

At the same time, given the uniqueness and idiosyncrasies of China's domestic market, many observers thought that overseas success of Chinese EV manufacturers was unlikely. For example, Teece (2018: 504) argued, "success in China, however, is not necessarily a good predictor of success globally." Yet the evidence has shown that Chinese automotive firms have multiple paths to globalization while developing both ordinary capabilities and dynamic capabilities. A notable example is Geely, which accelerated its globalization by acquiring Volvo Cars for $1.8 billion in 2010. Most remarkable is that in 2024 Chinese auto exports in unit terms surpassed those of any other country and have continued to grow in 2025.

The growing evidence also suggests that advances in technological capabilities and low-cost competitiveness by Chinese auto companies have given them the confidence to build plants overseas. For example, Chinese firms are targeting the geographically proximate Southeast Asian market: SAIC set up a new joint venture plant in Thailand, Geely acquired a 50 percent stake in a local Malaysian company, and BYD opened its first overseas automotive assembly plant in Thailand in 2024. Historically, these markets have been dominated by Japanese automakers, whose vehicles accounted for 86 percent of the market in Thailand in 2018. However, the structure of the market and consumer demand have greatly changed. Sales records for 2023 show that, with the exception of Tesla's Model Y and Model 3, the top ten EVs sold in Thailand were Chinese – among which BYD achieved particularly strong performance, comprising about 40 percent of the Thai EV market. The initial success of Chinese cars in Southeast Asia has been followed by success in Latin America, Africa, Central Asia, and Russia.

As mentioned earlier, battery technology is the key to the EV industry. A report by the European Union (Bielewski et al. 2023) states that, while Japan became the annual leader in battery patents in 2009, it lost this position after 2020, when South Korea and China took first and second place, respectively, as global leaders because of the gains by LG, CATL, and Samsung. At present, the main R&D competition is between South Korean and Chinese battery manufacturers and in 2024 the Chinese manufacturers had far surpassed the South Korean firms.[6]

These changes have been driven by the rapid pace of improvement in battery technology in terms of energy density, charging speed, driving range, and cost. As a result, the price of batteries dropped significantly, from $180/kWh in 2022 to $115/kWh in 2024, and is expected to $82/kWh by 2026 (Goldman Sachs 2024). This has led industry observers to predict that by 2026, EVs will achieve cost parity at time of sale with ICE vehicles even without government subsidies – by most measures, they are already cheaper on a life-cycle basis.[7] In 2025, over 20 percent of the global new car sales were only 4 percent, thirty-one countries have reached the point at which 5 percent of the new cars sold are EVs (Bloomberg News 2024). Among these countries, in Norway where in 2024 90 percent of the cars sold were EVs and in China in 2025 EVs accounted for more than 50 percent of the new cars sold.

The rise of EVs will not only help the world mitigate climate change but, more importantly, will shape the perspective on industrial transition, and the increasing competitiveness of EVs (projected and rapid price decreases, longevity, low operating costs, and superior performance) is likely to obsolete ICE technology across nearly all applications, perhaps, even including jet engines. For decades, many automakers believed that technologies such as fuel cells and hydrogen would prevail in any transition from the ICE and that the transition was likely to be slow[8] – in part because an entirely new energy distribution system would be needed. Something that electric vehicles did not need – all it needed was charging stations and a reworking of the electric grid – as the distribution system already existed.

The ICE manufacturers made half-hearted efforts to enter the EV market, but most (in particular, Toyota) were content to produce hybrids (see, e.g., McKinsey 2021; Wilmot 2023). This relatively benign neglect turned into a panic when they realized that Chinese firms, in the aggregate, had become the largest global producers of EVs (both passenger vehicles and buses) and an increasingly strong competitor in cutting-edge lithium battery technology and,

---

[6] www.iam-media.com/article/south-korea-most-likely-take-the-lead-in-lithium-ion-battery-race/.
[7] www.noahpinion.blog/p/evs-are-just-going-to-win/.
[8] www.scribd.com/document/35599785/Global-Auto-Executive-Survey-2010/.

just as important, had established an entire supply chain from lithium mining (China controls 80 percent of global production) to the design and assembly of EVs. And, most alarmingly, Chinese manufacturers were rapidly entering markets where automakers from the G-7 countries had traditionally been dominant.

In the 2020s, venture capital (VC) funding for EVs was at an all-time high.[9] According to the International Energy Agency (2022a), in the period 2018–2022, China accounted for 70 percent of VC investment in EV startups, whereas the United States led in investment in charging infrastructure, trucks, and battery components. IEA data also shows that, in 2022, VC investment in early-stage startups to develop battery technologies increased 15 percent over the level in 2021, totaling nearly $850 million. In 2023, funding for new EV entrants seemed to dry up, as competition intensified, and major ICE manufacturers accelerated production of EVs (IEA 2023), and this retreat by investors continued in 2025.

The consulting firm, AlixPartners, estimated that by 2025 investment in EVs would reach a cumulative total $330 billion. Reuters stated that global automakers expect to spend over one and a half trillion dollars on EVs and batteries until 2030 (Lienert 2022). These investments reflected the looming urgency of addressing zero-carbon mandates in cities such as London and Paris and countries from Norway to China, though by 2024 venture capitalists and many European and US incumbents began to postpone or cancel their planned investment as the market for their EVs did not materialize as they had expected.

At the time that this Element was being finalized, the advance of the EV industry in China was making ICE automobiles obsolete there, and, given the growth in the market and advances in technology, China is almost certain to lead the world in the global transition to EVs. But it is also possible that the period of technological ferment is not over and that other energy-storage technologies might replace lithium-based battery technologies. However, at present, the technological trajectory toward lithium, and possibly sodium batteries, in which Chinese firms are increasingly dominant, appears likely to continue.

We draw on evidence from extensive internet searches, including public documents, company histories, and other archival data. By triangulating various resources (articles in business newspapers, consulting reports, trade journals, publicly available interviews and presentations, etc.), we chronicle the emergence and evolution in China's EV industry, which began with earlier initiatives in five-year plans (FYPs) and was dramatically initiated with the country's ninth FYP (1996–2000) and highlighted during the twelfth FYP (2011–2015).

---

[9] www.atlasevhub.com/weekly-digest/u-s-leads-other-countries-in-announced-ev-manufacturing-investments/.

Since the enactment in the United States of both the CHIPS (Creating Helpful Incentives to Produce Semiconductors) and Science Act in 2022 and the Inflation Reduction Act (IRA) in 2023, US auto manufacturers planned to quadruple their announced EV manufacturing and battery investment to $210 billion, which was expected to exceed that of any other country (Mui 2023). Moreover, because of the success of Chinese EV firms, in 2024 and, more recently, under Trump the US government wanted to impose heavy tariffs in order to protect the US market against imports of Chinese EVs. As part of the legislation, the US government intends to exclude Chinese battery firms and even licensing of their global-leading technologies by US manufacturers – and Korean and Japanese battery makers hoped to take advantage of this, though again their involvement is likely contingent upon the new Trump administration's decisions.

The Element begins by discussing the history of EVs. At the beginning of the automobile era, several different battery-powered vehicles were developed yet failed to prevail, as the ICE won out due to technical challenges and the cooperation between automakers and the petroleum industry, which rapidly built out a fuel infrastructure. We then fast-forward to the twenty-first century to discuss the experimentation and reemergence of EVs in the form of the Chevy Volt and the Nissan Leaf, followed by the emergence and success of Tesla. Then we explore the interaction between government policy and entrepreneurial activity that led to the emergence and rise to global dominance of China's EV industry.

Next, we show that the Chinese EV industry is based on the building of an EV supplier ecosystem that increasingly integrates the entire value chain from raw materials mining to recycling – a process that made China the center of the EV global industry. The ferocious competition in China resulted in excess capacity and dramatic price decreases and has driven EV manufacturers, domestic and foreign, to export automobiles, as discussed in Section 5. Subsequently, China became the world's largest automobile exporter, and Chinese EV firms are establishing manufacturing operations globally. We offer reflections on China's success and its implications for the global economy.

The Element concludes with a discussion of the implications of this profound technological disruption and paradigm change. How will it affect China and its economy? Does this transition in the transportation industry have a positive effect on what some have called China's middle-income trap (Lewin et al. 2016)? Are batteries the next main general-purpose technology? If advancement in battery technology and Chinese centrality in EV production continues, in combination with the powerful position of Chinese firms in photovoltaics, wind turbines, and other alternative energy technologies, will China lead the energy transition globally? Could the EV transition in China enable it to lead the next Kondratieff long wave? Will this enable China to become the global center, not just of manufacturing but of the global economy in general? Finally, will this transition cause the United States, Japan, and Western Europe to become clean technology backwaters? Certainly, much is at stake in the EV revolution.

2 The Early History of Battery-Powered Cars

2.1 Early Experimentation in Battery-Powered Cars by ICE Innovators

Experimentation using electric motors to propel vehicles can be traced back to the early nineteenth century. There was continuing experimentation, and in the 1830s, Robert Anderson, a Scottish inventor, created the first electric carriage, which was powered by power cells that could not be charged. During the next half-century, rechargeable batteries were developed and continually improved. Various technological developments led to the formation of a "horseless carriage industry" in the United States and Europe that was characterized by lively competition among three different propulsion technologies: internal combustion, steam, and electrical power. In 1887, in the United States, William Morrison, a Scottish-born chemist introduced an early EV that had front-wheel drive and a top speed of 20 miles per hour. In the years that followed, EVs from various automakers began to appear in cities across the United States.

One of the first significant electric automobiles in the United States was invented and patented by Henry G. Morris and Pedro G. Salom in 1894. The patent and firm were then sold to Isaac L. Rice, and he changed its name from the Electric Storage Battery Company to the Electric Vehicle Company (EVC), which, by the early 1900s, had over 600 electric taxis operating on the East Coast. Unsurprisingly, electric car pioneers and electrical companies already faced the recharging problem and, in at least one case, created a collective action solution by launching a battery-swapping service as a solution to increase the driving range of early rudimentary EVs. This problem persisted with EVs and in the 2000s the same problem was addressed by the Silicon Valley startup Better Place with its "battery switching" service and then by NIO in China, which also introduced battery switching as its business model for solving the "refilling" problem.

In 1888, William Warren Gibbs founded the Electric Storage Battery Company, after having purchased the ideas and patents of inventor Clement Payen to commercialize the storage battery. Gibbs targeted electric lighting companies, which could use the batteries to offer electrical power to their customers. In 1894, Gibbs announced the acquisition of the intellectual property rights of the General Electric

Company, the Edison Company, the Thomson-Houston Company, the Accumulator Company, the Consolidated Electric Storage Company, and the General Electric Launch Company. In 1900 the Electric Storage Battery Company introduced a battery with higher capacity and significantly lower weight for electric taxicabs and renamed the company Exide, an abbreviation of "excellent oxide." Exide then joined with Pope, a pioneer in gasoline-powered vehicles, and began to manufacture and sell EVs. Eventually, they produced 1,000 vehicles – well before the ICE producers in Detroit attained large-scale production.

Europe and the United States experienced a burst of automotive innovation in the late nineteenth and early twentieth centuries, though the market for cars remained limited. Importantly, a period of ferment about which energy source would power horseless carriages followed. Even some of the pioneers, such as Ransom Olds (Oldsmobile) and Ferdinand Porsche, marketed battery-powered vehicles. An American coachbuilder, Studebaker manufactured wagons and later automobiles; it entered the rapidly growing automotive industry in 1902 with a battery-powered electric car and then in 1904 introduced gasoline-powered cars, which it marketed as the Studebaker Automobile Company.

Although ICE cars began to dominate the market for automobiles, EVs held on to their market share, especially in cities where their silent operation and ease of use appealed to mainly affluent buyers. However, on October 1, 1908, the Ford Motor Company began production of its Model T (popularly known as the Tin Lizzie), the first ICE automobile produced for the masses at a low cost. The price was $780 in 1910 but fell to $290 by 1924 ($5,156 in 2023 dollars). Over 15 million Model Ts were sold, and only was surpassed in 1972 by the Volkswagen Beetle. The Model T was so successful because it offered inexpensive transportation built on a highly efficient assembly line and symbolized the rise in economic status of the middle class as well as the age of modernization in the United States. It sealed the fate of EVs. And, as importantly, the petroleum companies led by Standard Oil began a national buildout of "filling stations," solving the refueling problem.

2.2 EVs and Hybrid Car Development Beginning in the 1990s, Mostly in Japan

During the energy crises of 1973–1974 and 1979, the price of gasoline soared, and the debate about diversifying energy sources for transportation was rekindled, but when the price of gasoline fell again, the debate waned. In the 1990s, interest in alternative energy sources reemerged, driven in part by increases in automobile fleet efficiency regulatory requirements and the acrid pollution that enveloped US cities. In 1996, GM introduced the EV1Insert, leading to a comeback in "mass-produced" EVs, as shown by the popularity of GM

Bolt. However, in 2002 GM discontinued it, in favor of its concept car, the Impact, which used conventional lead acid batteries and had a range of about 55 miles (Mom 2013).

Other initiatives included Honda's introduction in 1999 of its experimental EV, the Honda EV Plus, which had a range of 81 miles. The Nissan Leaf was probably the most successful EV sold by an ICE manufacturer, and in November 2009 *Time* magazine listed it as one of the "50 Best Inventions" of that year. In December 2010, under the leadership of Carlos Ghosn, its CEO at the time, Nissan put the Leaf, with a range of 100 miles per charge, on sale in the United States and Japan. Other attempts at EV innovation by ICE manufacturers included the Mitsubishi i-MiEV and the Honda Fit.

All the ICE manufacturers recognized the potential of EVs, yet, as a GM spokesperson claimed in the documentary *Who Killed the Electric Car?*, "We spent over $1 billion over four years and were only able to lease 800 EV1s," demonstrating the lack of traction gained by the early EVs. The high price gap between PHEVs and EVs also led consumers to prefer the former. In 2010, the Mitsubishi i-MiEV went on sale at a price of $47,000, which, even after the $7,500 subsidy per vehicle in the United States, was still expensive. By comparison, NiMH-powered hybrids, such as the Toyota Prius and Honda Insight, were listed at around $23,000 and $20,000, respectively, which was below the average price of $24,296 for a new car sold in the United States in 2010. Toyota, in particular, was content with the sales of its hybrid vehicle, the Prius. The Prius project began as a learning project to develop Toyota's manufacturing capabilities based on the production of the ICE.[10] Since 1997, when the Prius was released, the growth in hybrids was remarkable, with 33.4 million sold in 2023 alone, making it the world's best-selling hybrid. On December 19, 2022, Akio Toyoda, then the CEO of Toyota, reportedly claimed that EVs were not the only way forward for the auto industry and that a "silent majority" in the (ICE) auto industry agreed.[11]

---

[10] Based on Shu (2022), the origins of the Prius can be traced back to 1993, when Eiji Toyota, then chairman of the company at the time, expressed concern about Toyota's future growth. In response, the then-vice president in charge of research and development approved the "G21 (Global 21st century) project" to develop a new compact car with improved fuel efficiency for internal combustion engines. The engineering team proposed what they believed to be the best solution at the time: to improve fuel efficiency by 50% compared to Toyota's best-selling compact car, the Corolla, to a level of 47.5 miles per gallon. However, this proposal was rejected by the management team, who believed that it was not enough to simply improve the fuel efficiency of the internal combustion engine by 50%. This led to the development of the hybrid car, the Prius.

[11] www.businessinsider.com/toyota-electric-cars-ceo-hybrids-plug-in-silent-majority-resistance-2022-12/.

Toyota led the "hybrid revolution" and was followed by other ICE vehicle manufacturers. Some of them argued that hybrids were a transition technology to an electric future. In particular, Toyota has long pursued an "all-around" strategy involving all alternatives (such as fuel cells), and did not focus on EVs. For example, as late as 2023, the Toyota's chief scientist called for not transitioning too quickly to EVs, arguing that hybrids should have more time to develop. Although Toyota is the world's most profitable car company, its EV sales in 2023 accounted for only 1 percent of its global sales. As Clayton Christensen (2013) might have predicted, ICE automakers, especially Toyota, did not drive the transition to a new technological paradigm. That fell to new entrants: Tesla and the Chinese EV firms.[12]

2.3 And Then Came Tesla

Entrepreneurs have a long history of interest in EVs. The firm with the largest impact was Tesla, which was founded in 2003 to commercialize EVs (Stringham et al. 2015). Tesla entered the auto industry by first retrofitting an ICE vehicle with batteries and an electric motor (Perkins & Murmann 2018), relying on partnerships with firms such as Panasonic, at that time, the main battery maker for Toyota's hybrids. Tesla also benefited from its ability to sell energy efficiency credits to existing automakers as well as massive subsidies from the federal and local governments (Hirsch 2015).

In 2012, Tesla entered the mainstream with the introduction of its second model, the S sedan, followed by other models, which were rapidly adopted by consumers. Tesla's success, which became apparent after 2015, forced other automakers to reckon with the market for EVs. Even then, however, Tesla (as well as other smaller EV startups, e.g., Fisker, Lucid, and Rivian) was still regarded as serving only a niche market. Nevertheless, by the late 2010s, Tesla had become the most valuable car company in the world. Although Tesla had rapidly matured as an auto manufacturer, it continued to depend on Asian battery producers for the design and, just as important, production of batteries, which meant that the R&D and production of this crucial component remained largely in Asia.[13] Tesla's world leadership in manufacturing EVs ended in 2024, when BYD took the lead.

The decision by legacy ICE firms not to aggressively pursue EVs and, in particular, the huge success of Toyota's Prius became a hindrance for it, in particular, from fully shifting its focus to EVs, although Toyota repeatedly

---

[12] There were a number of other US EV startups, including Fisker, Rivian, Lucid, and yet others, but all of these have failed or are close to failure.

[13] For example, Tesla's Gigafactory in Nevada was built and operated by Panasonic, and SK Battery built a factory in Georgia.

claimed that "hybrid technology can navigate the transitional period toward electrification." Toyota's hesitation and the hope for the durability of hybrids opened the way for Tesla to become the global EV leader. Effectively, Tesla and its charismatic leader, Elon Musk, proved that there was a global market for EVs and initiated the building of an EV supply chain, although until the 2010s it remained a small niche producer. Some European legacy ICE automakers, prompted by government policies aimed at achieving a carbon-neutral future, also began to make EVs. However, it was in China that a paradigm shift was successfully achieved through a gathering momentum and an increasingly powerful shift toward the development and manufacturing of EVs to meet the demands of the rapidly growing Chinese market. This was driven by a synergy of government policies and unique China bottom-up entrepreneurial initiatives and inter-provincial competition.

3 The Rise of the Chinese EV Industry

3.1 Evolution of China's Industrial Policy in New Energy Vehicles

Given China's long-term dependence on petroleum imports, it is not surprising that the Chinese government began to consider NEVs by the 1980s. Further, as the Chinese economy grew and Chinese cities boomed, the country experienced a dramatic and health-threatening increase in air pollution, in large measure, due to ICE automobiles. This added incentive to the search for new non-petroleum-based transportation solutions. For example, in 1990, the eighth National Key Technology R&D Program supported small-scale EV demonstration projects. Government interest in NEVs was also heightened by the fact that the joint ventures with Western multinational enterprises that were ICE automakers resulted in only minimal technology transfer, and yet, generated enormous profits (Helveston et al. 2019). The government came to understand that the foreign firms had no interest in improving the capabilities of their Chinese JV partners – and it became clear that it would take a long time to catch up to them in manufacturing ICE (Howell 2018).

This section focuses on the central government policies regarding NEVs, while recognizing that many of these policies were delegated to the local and provincial governments, resulting in a large variety of incentives directed at both NEV producers and consumers. For example, Shenzhen assisted BYD by purchasing EV-powered municipal buses (Ren 2018). The municipal government of Shanghai was very important in assisting Tesla in its negotiations over obtaining an operating license for its wholly owned Gigafactory there (Han 2024). Local government initiative in developing bottom-up strategies is a central aspect of the Chinese national innovation system (Sun & Kenney

2024). However, in the interest of brevity, we do not include local government policies, though they have been vital in nurturing the growth of NEV firms and technologies – and, in many cases, local governments, through their interaction with local firms (e.g., BYD and the Shenzhen local government), learn and develop policies before the central government (Sun & Kenney 2024).

Government policy concerning NEVs can be separated into several stages of development. Initially, the government discussion and policy initiatives were largely R&D oriented and rather general. Later, central government attention increasingly was directed to EVs and developing an entire ecosystem, including suppliers, and even going so far as to secure access to key raw materials, rollout a charging infrastructure, and even end-of-life recycling. At each stage, R&D was encouraged and incentives were provided to build an entire supply chain. In the following discussion, we divide this development process to reflect these stages.

3.1.1 Stage 1: Industrial Policies for Developing the Technology, 2001–2009

Although experimentation was already underway, the tenth five-year plan (FYP) for National Economic and Social Development, released in 2001, explicitly called for "the development of economical cars, the improvement of the manufacturing level of automobiles and key components, and the active development of high-efficiency, energy-saving and low-emission automobile engines and hybrid power systems."[14] During this period, the idea of developing an "NEV industry" started to appear in various "horizontal" national key industrial planning and policy documents, though, at this time, there were very few industry-specific dedicated policies. From 2001 to 2009, the central government industry policies mainly targeted the development of technology that would enable a NEV industry to emerge – also, at this time, the R&D incentives were technology agnostic (i.e., EV, hybrid, or fuel cell/hydrogen).

In 2001, the State Economic and Trade Commission issued the tenth FYP for the Automobile Industry, calling for the promotion of "R&D of electric and hybrid vehicles, accelerate the popularization and use of alternative-fuel vehicles, and proceed with the leapfrog development of the automobile industry."[15] This FYP was important, as it explicitly called for the development and commercialization of NEVs. In addition to the horizontal policy stress, the central government promoted the initiation of the NEV industry by launching the 863 Major Special R&D Program of the Ministry of Science and Technology (MoST) on Energy-saving and New Energy Vehicles, which

---

[14] www.gov.cn/gongbao/content/2001/content_60699.htm.
[15] https://gdii.gd.gov.cn/zcgh3227/content/post_937864.html.

jumpstarted R&D investment in NEVs. To pursue the development of NEVs, the central government announced the "three vertical and three horizontal" technology development strategy, building on a policy direction that had started in the 1990s. The "three vertical and three horizontal" means the three vertical vehicle technology routes, that is, "hybrid vehicles, pure electric vehicles, and fuel cell vehicles"; and the three horizontal system routes, that is, "the multi-energy powertrain control system, the electric drive motor and control system, and the power storage battery system."[16] This policy nurtured the development of the fundamental technologies that supported subsequent development of China's NEV industry.

Subsequently, a series of technology development measures were announced. In February 2003, the General Office of the State Economic and Trade Commission formally released the Notice on Declaring the National Technology Innovation Plan Projects, declaring NEVs and related technologies and products as an area in which firms could apply for project support. Then, in December 2005, the National Development and Reform Commission (NDRC) (including the former National Development Planning Commission, the former National Planning Commission) launched the Industrial Structure Adjustment Guidance Catalogue (2005), adding "the development and manufacturing of new energy vehicles (e.g., hybrid cars, electric cars, fuel cell vehicles) and their key components." At the same time, the State Council issued the "National Medium and Long-term Science and Technology Development Plan Outline (2006–2020)" declaring that the national key areas and priority themes included "low energy consumption and new energy vehicles."[17]

One year later, the Eleventh FYP for the Development of Science and Technology called for the organization and implementation of major projects on energy saving and NEVs in the plan for the development of modern transportation technology.[18] The development of energy saving and new energy vehicles was included in the "Outline for the Implementation of International Science and Technology Cooperation in the Eleventh Five-Year Plan" and the notice on "The Key Technologies and Product Catalogs that China should master Indigenous Intellectual Property Rights" in late 2006. These policies emphasize the development of energy-saving and new energy vehicles, comprising the development of technologies for complete vehicle design; integration and manufacturing; power system integration and control; an automotive computing platform; key components, such as high-efficiency and low-emission ICEs, fuel-cell engines, power batteries, and drive motors; and NEV

---

[16] www.most.gov.cn/xxgk/xinxifenlei/fdzdgknr/fgzc/zcjd/202106/t20210628_175505.html.
[17] www.gov.cn/gongbao/content/2006/content_240244.htm.
[18] www.most.gov,cb/ztzl/qgkjgzhy/2007/2007syw/200701/t20070124_39953.htm.

infrastructure.[19] In late 2007, the NDRC released the "Management Rules for Access to New Energy Vehicle Production and Industrial Restructuring Guidance Catalog (2007)" defining NEVs and outlining specific requirements for firms that wanted to qualify for, access, and apply for government support.[20]

In the tenth FYP period, the central government invested RMB 880 million (about US$125 million) in the "863" Electric Vehicle Major Science and Technology Project to support automobile manufacturers and universities that wished to form partnerships to develop technology. Then, in the eleventh FYP period, the government funded 270 science and technology projects on NEVs based on the "863" Energy-Saving and New Energy Vehicle R&D Major Project, which covered key components, power systems, vehicle integration, test platforms, demonstration and promotion, as well as standards and policies. The financial investment available through the project totaled RMB 7.5 billion, of which RMB 1.16 billion was allocated out of central government financing, and more than RMB 7.5 billion was invested by local governments and enterprises.[21] During this period, the main emphasis was on technology development across all NEV technologies. Tesla was formed in Silicon Valley to develop EVs in 2003; thus, China was using government-funded university/industry partnerships to develop NEV technology at roughly the same time that global leaders such as Tesla were being founded, and hybrid vehicles, in particular, the Prius, achieved significant market acceptance. At roughly the same time as these developments, though largely unsupervised or supported by the government, Chinese entrepreneurs were introducing battery-powered motorcycles that were successful with consumers (Weinert 2007) and learning from these developments. As this phase ended, the central government began to consider the demonstration phase.

3.1.2 Stage 2: Industrial Policy for Pilot Production, 2009–2013

Beginning in 2009, the government introduced policies to create a market for NEVs. The central government began by designating pilot cities that would create demand for NEVs. These industrial policies were a combination of short-term demonstration projects and medium- and long-term plans. In early 2009, the State Council advocated the large-scale development of NEVs and called for large-scale demonstration pilot projects. The centerpiece was the "Ten Cities and One Thousand Vehicles Demonstration and Application Project for Energy Saving and New Energy Vehicles," known as the Ten Cities and One Thousand

---

[19] www.gov.cn/jrzg/2006-12/03/content_460262.htm; www.lawtime.cn/info/zscq/guojiazhengcefagui/2010110951412.html.
[20] www.mofcom.gov.cn/aarticle/b/g/200712/20071205290556.html.
[21] www.gov.cn/jrzg/2012-09/14/content_2224960.htm.

Vehicles Policy. This policy initiative was jointly introduced by the MoST, the Ministry of Finance (MoF), the NDRC, and the Ministry of Industry and Information Technology (MIIT). The policy assigned financial subsidies to 10 cities annually in three-year windows.[22] Each city was meant to purchase and use 1,000 NEVs. These large and medium-size cities introduced NEVs in various fields, including public transportation (NEV buses), rentals, public service vehicles, and postal services. The ambitious goal was to have NEVs account for 10 percent of all vehicles sold by 2012. However, in 2012, only 27,432 pilot vehicles were in use in the 25 NEV demonstration cities – of which 23,032 were in the public service sector and 4,400 were purchased by private individuals (Wang et al. 2012). The results of these initial demonstration cities were disappointing. Only 40 percent of the target for the public service sector fleet for the twenty-five cities was attained (Gong et al. 2013). Moreover, in 2012, only seven cities had 1,000 NEVs in operation (Economy 2014).

Also in 2009, the State Council issued the "Plan for the Adjustment and Revitalization of the Automobile Industry" to announce that it would invest RMB 10 billion (US $1.25 billion) to support NEV manufacturing and the production of key components. EVs were highlighted in this plan, which stated goals such as:

> Scaling the electric vehicles' production and sales. Transforming the existing production capacity to form 500,000 new energy vehicles (pure electric, rechargeable hybrid, and ordinary hybrid) production capacity. Having new energy vehicle sales account for about 5 percent of total passenger car sales. Major passenger car manufacturers should have certified new energy vehicle products.[23]

In 2010, the State Council (2010) declared that NEVs were among China's seven strategic key emerging industries according to the industrial policy.[24]

---

[22] In 2009, thirteen major cities were approved by the central government as the pilots executing the "Ten Cities and One Thousand Vehicles Policy," involving Beijing, Shanghai, Shenzhen, Wuhan, Hangzhou, Chongqing, Changchun, Dalian, Jinan, Hefei, Changsha, Kunming, and Nanchang; one year later, the National Development and Reform Commission, the Ministry of Industry and Information Technology, the Ministry of Finance and the Ministry of Science and Technology jointly approved the second phase of seven pilot cities, involving Tianjin, Haikou, Zhengzhou, Xiamen, Suzhou, Tangshan and Guangzhou; then in 2011, another five pilot cities of the third phase were approved, including Shenyang, Huhehaote, Chengdu, Nantong, Xiangyang. In total, these twenty-five pilot cities held more than 30 percent of the country's vehicle ownership at the time. Five of these twenty-five cities (i.e., Shanghai, Changchun, Shenzhen, Hangzhou, and Hefei) were also designated as frontier pilots for the development private new energy vehicle market (from report Driving a Green Future. China's Electric Vehicle Development Review and Future Outlook).

[23] www.gov.cn/zhengce/zhengceku/2009-03/20/content_8121.htm.

[24] The State Council determined China's seven strategic key emerging industries as follows: energy-saving and environmental protection industry, new generation information technology

The Decision of the State Council on Accelerating the Cultivation and Development of Strategic Emerging Industries was quite comprehensive, specifically targeting:

> Breakthroughs in key core technologies in the fields of power batteries, drive motors, and electronic control, and promote the popularization, application, and industrialization of plug-in hybrid and pure electric vehicles. At the same time, carrying out research and development of cutting-edge technologies related to fuel cell vehicles, and vigorously promote the development of energy-efficient and low-emission energy-saving vehicles.[25]

Other policies regarding financial subsidies and specific product categories were issued as well, such as the Interim Measures for the Administration of Financial Subsidies for the Demonstration and Promotion of Energy-saving and New Energy Vehicles in 2009,[26] the Implementing Rules for the Promotion of Energy-Efficient Vehicles (Passenger Cars Below 1.6 Liters) under the Energy-Efficient Products Benefiting the People Project in 2010,[27] and the Notice on the Adjustment of Subsidy Policies for the Promotion of Energy-Efficient Vehicles in 2011.[28]

In 2012, the State Council followed up by launching the Development Plan for Energy-saving and New Energy Vehicle Industry (2012–2020) further clarifying the technology trajectory of China's NEV industry as

> targeting pure electric drive as the main strategic orientation for the development of new energy vehicles and the transformation of the automobile industry, the current focus is on promoting the industrialization of pure electric vehicles and plug-in hybrid vehicles, promoting the popularization of non-plug-in hybrid vehicles and energy-saving internal combustion engine vehicles, and upgrading the overall technical level of China's automobile industry.[29]

Interestingly, this 2012 policy shows that EVs and PHEVs were becoming the focus of government policies for industrialization, as hybrids such as the Prius and energy-efficient ICE vehicles were being accepted in the market. However, the policy clearly acknowledges that the Chinese automobile industry technically continued to lag the overall global level, especially in hybrids and energy-efficient ICE vehicles.

---

industry, biology industry, high-end equipment manufacturing industry, new energy industry, new materials industry, and new energy automobile industry.
[25] www.gov.cn/gongbao/content/2010/content_1730695.htm.
[26] www.gov.cn/zwgk/2009-02/05/content_1222338.htm.
[27] www.gov.cn/gzdt/2010-06/02/content_1619223.htm.
[28] www.ndrc.gov.cn/fggz/hjyzy/zyzhlyhxhjj/201109/t20110920_1315265.html.
[29] www.gov.cn/gongbao/content/2012/content_2182749.htm.

The government recognized that NEV industrialization still required significant preparation and policy mobilization. The Development Plan for the Energy-Saving and New Energy Vehicle Industry (2012–2020) set a goal that "by 2015, the cumulative production and sales volume of pure electric vehicles and plug-in hybrid vehicles will strive to reach 500,000 units; and by 2020, the production capacity of pure electric vehicles and plug-in hybrid vehicles will reach 2 million units, and the cumulative production and sales volume will exceed 5 million units."[30]

By 2012, the Chinese government had clearly identified EV and PHEV as the goal of its NEV policy. To calibrate Chinese development, the interest in EVs was growing rapidly as new EV firms were being formed in the United States and, in particular, Tesla was growing rapidly. Further, Chinese air pollution problems were worsening, as automobile ownership grew rapidly. To achieve widespread adoption of NEVs, the government decided that new policies to encourage their purchase were needed.

3.1.3 Stage 3: Industrial Policy for Large-Scale Adoption, 2013–2018

In the third stage, the government goal was to target the large-scale adoption of NEVs. First, the Ten Cities and One Thousand Vehicles Policy was extended due to an evaluation of NEV promotion programs in various cities by several ministries and confirmed 39 cities/city clusters as the basis for this promotion of NEVs between 2013 and 2014 – this included most of China's large and medium-size cities. By September 2015, 180,945 NEVs were operating in 39 cities. Moreover, in 2015, 379,000 NEVs were sold, outpacing US EV sales. Going forward, China became the world's largest NEV market (Liu 2024: 37).

Industrial policies now focused on consumption incentives to encourage large-scale adoption. For example, implementation of the purchase tax exemption policy in September 2014 triggered rapid adoption by individuals. The central government introduced purchase subsidies, such as the "Announcement About the Purchase Tax Exemption of New Energy Vehicles,"[31] the "Implementation Plan for Government Agencies and Public Institutions Purchasing New Energy Vehicles,"[32] and the "Notice on Issues About the Electricity Price Policy for Electric Vehicles."[33] For example, in the Financial Support Policies for the Promotion and Application of New Energy Vehicles for the Period 2016–2020 issued in 2015 that targeted consumers. NEV manufacturers reduced the price of

---

[30] www.gov.cn/gongbao/content/2012/content_2182749.htm.
[31] http://tjtb.mofcom.gov.cn/article/e/201408/20140800690450.shtml.
[32] www.gov.cn/xinwen/2014-07/13/content_2716565.htm.
[33] http://jgs.ndrc.gov.cn/zcfg/201408/t20140801_621052.html.

vehicles by deducting the subsidies, and the central government reimbursed manufacturers.[34] In addition, the subsidy was based on the vehicle's energy savings, emissions reduction, and other factors, such as the production cost, production scale, and technology level. The policy set the subsidy standard in 2016 for various types of NEVs. In 2017–2020, subsidies other than those for fuel cell vehicles were gradually reduced. For example, the level of subsidy for NEVs in 2016 was reduced in 2017–2018 by 20 percent and in 2019–2020 by another 20 percent over the level in 2016 (Liu 2024: 109).

The government also advocated subnational industrial policies, such as preferential license quotas, traffic control exemptions, and infrastructure support. Many cities addressed the infrastructure bottlenecks by increasing the installation of public chargers. In addition, some cities reduced costs for vehicle owners by reducing annual inspection fees and parking fees, among other policies. For example, in 2014 the Beijing government drastically reduced the new ICE vehicle quotas, while increasing those for NEVs.

At the same time, to increase the size of the NEV market the central government introduced vertically specific industrial policies such as restricting licenses for ICE vehicles, except for the zero-emissions EVs and implementing policies to accelerate the large-scale NEV adoption. For example, the Measures for Parallel Management of Average Fuel Consumption and New Energy Vehicle Points for Passenger Vehicle Enterprises were launched on September 27, 2017.[35] In this document, the MIIT and other five departments jointly established two types of points for average fuel consumption and NEVs of enterprises and established a point trading mechanism that enterprises could use for independently determining how to offset negative points and thereby achieve two goals: energy conservation and reduction in fossil fuel consumption as well as NEV development.

These approaches enabled rapid growth in the consumer market for NEVs, as the number grew from a few thousand in the public transportation niche at the end of 2013 to more than 60,000 at the end of 2017, of which more than 60 percent are privately owned (Jin et al. 2021). This trend is shown in Figure 4. The growth was disrupted in 2016, when a scandal regarding NEV subsidy frauds erupted, as five NEV manufacturers were producing and selling poorly made EVs to car rental firms that they owned and then collected over RMB 1 billion (approximately $150 million) in public subsidies (Yan & Dou 2016). As a result, it was announced that fiscal incentives would be gradually decreased. Also, in the future, to qualify for subsidies, NEVs would have to be graded by government inspectors, and the subsidies would favor EVs with advanced technologies.

---

[34] www.miit.gov.cn/jgsj/zbes/gzdt/art/2020/art_dc795b036a644bdf8e3e38a75107c401.html.
[35] www.gov.cn/zhengce/2022-11/27/content_5722693.htm.

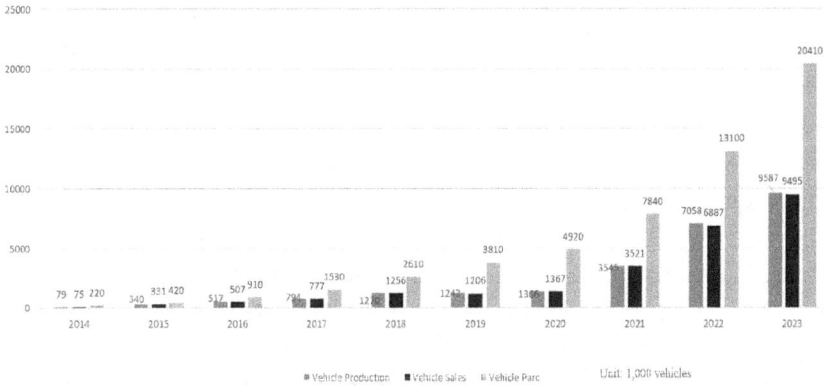

Figure 4 Production, sales, and registration of China's new energy vehicles (2014–2023)
Source: China Association of Automobile Manufacturers.

Finally, anti-fraud and enforcement measures were added that allowed government officials to test and certify NEVs (Qiong 2017). These measures initiated a new phase of deeper government involvement in the NEV market.

3.1.4 Stage 4: Industrial Policy to Encourage Market Competition, 2018–

In this fourth stage, which began in early 2018, the central government gradually decreased the subsidies and promoted the marketization of NEVs. In February 2018, the four ministries (i.e., MoST, MoF, NDRC, MIIT) jointly issued the Notice on Adjusting and Improving Financial Subsidy Policies for the Promotion and Application of New Energy Vehicles, highlighting the increase in technical threshold requirements, raising the standards to qualify for subsidies, and increasing the driving range for NEVs.[36] Also, it was decided that subsidy policies would be updated annually and gradually decreased in terms of the size and the vehicles that qualified. Contemporaneously, the government opened the Chinese market by allowing the then global leader, Tesla, to build a factory in China in a bid to further spur competition. In July 2018, the Shanghai Municipal Government and Tesla signed a memorandum of cooperation to build a factory wholly owned by Tesla meant to produce 500,000 EVs per year.

The central government also increased support for building charging infrastructure and deploying batteries, and so forth, while encouraging technological innovation in NEVs, such as developing intelligent, connected vehicles. The

---

[36] www.gov.cn/xinwen/2016-12/30/content_5154971.htm#1/.

Circular of the General Office of the State Council on the Issuance of the New Energy Vehicle Industry Development Plan (2021–2035) issued by the State Council highlights focusing the development agenda on the "three vertical and three horizontal" R&D trajectories. With respect to the "three vertical" trajectories, it emphasized focusing on pure electric vehicles, plug-in hybrid (including programmable) vehicles, and fuel cell vehicles. In addition, the industrial policy emphasizes improving EV infrastructure by subsidizing the construction of charging networks, coordinating and promoting the construction of intelligent road networks and facilitates, and orderly creation of a hydrogen fuel supply system.[37]

Since the 10th FYP for the National Economic and Social Development of China, China's NEV industrial policy has evolved in four stages. The initial "three vertical and three horizontal" technology development strategy was intended to develop the technology for building a domestic NEV industry. The targets of these industrial policies evolved from the supply side to the demand side. Initially, the demand-side industrial policies were aimed at vehicles for public transportation, such as buses and taxis, in designated cities. This was followed by attempts at large-scale marketization of NEVs in the nationwide consumer market for passenger cars. This stage was driven by production and sales subsidies. In this stage, the supply-side industrial policies continued, with large subsidies for R&D and the development of charging infrastructure. The interactions between the supply-side and demand-side industrial policies contributed to the ongoing evolution of NEVs. When technological capabilities (e.g., battery technological innovations by CATL and BYD), production levels, and the scale (e.g., large sales) satisfied the conditions for industrialization, the competitive advantage of China's EV industry began to fully emerge.

3.2 Building the Chinese EV Industry: Bottom-up Entrepreneurial Activities

The various NEV policies by the Chinese government set the stage for the development of the EV industry. However, the technology and industry transition might not have been possible in the absence of entrepreneurial entry and the evolution of an intensely competitive industry. This section briefly highlights the emergence of the startup EV companies and provides a historical sketch of two leading Chinese EV companies – BYD, NIO – and the leading battery company, CATL. This section also provides an overview of other startups and highlights the emerging nature of China's EV industry as a result of the creative

---

[37] www.mee.gov.cn/zcwj/gwywj/202011/t20201103_806156.shtml.

disruption of existing technological paths by the large number of new entrants and the entrepreneurial spirit to discover new opportunities in the growing EV market.

3.2.1 BYD

In a 2011 interview with Bloomberg, Elon Musk was asked whether he considered BYD, which had just received a large investment from Warren Buffett's investment firm, Berkshire Hathaway, a competitor. He responded that BYD was not competent enough to be a competitor because "[they do] not yet [have] a very strong technology, and their focus should be making sure that they don't die in China." Ten years later, in 2023, when he was asked about this interview, he replied on his Twitter feed, "That was many years ago. Their cars are extremely competitive." That year, BYD surpassed Tesla as the top-selling NEV manufacturer worldwide.[38]

BYD's history can be traced back to 1995, when it was founded by Wang Chuanfu in Shenzhen as a rechargeable battery company. Before founding BYD, Wang – who had a master's degree in metallurgical physics and chemistry – worked at a state-owned research institute as a researcher. Initially, BYD competed with Sanyo, the dominant player in the OEM rechargeable battery market, by offering low-price products. BYD quickly replaced Sanyo as a supplier to Daba, Taiwan's largest manufacturer of cordless telephones.

In 1997, when a financial crisis swept Southeast Asia, and most Japanese battery makers experienced rising labor costs, BYD expanded its market share by offering lower-cost batteries. In 2000, BYD became the first Chinese supplier of lithium-ion batteries to be certified by Motorola. Two years later, BYD became Nokia's first Chinese battery supplier. BYD's sales, which relied on lower prices, grew to RMB 100 million ($12.5 million) by 2003, and it became the world's second-largest producer of rechargeable batteries.

What, in retrospect, was a fateful decision occurred in January 2003. Wang decided to go into the automobile industry by acquiring a 77 percent stake in Xi'an Qinchuan Automobile Co. With this purchase, BYD became China's second private automaker, after Geely. In 2005, the BYD F3, powered by a Mitsubishi 1.6 L engine, was introduced on the emerging Chinese domestic auto market. The success of the BYD F3 was due to its cost performance. Its stylish appearance and configuration resembled those of the Toyota Corolla, but its price was only RMB 73,800, almost half the price of a Corolla. The F3 quickly became popular, with 63,153 sold in 2006.

---

[38] www.bydglobal.com/en/news/2024-07-04/BYD-Thailand-Factory-Inauguration-and-Roll-off-of-Its-8-Millionth-New-Energy-Vehicle/.

This resulted in the development of one of BYD's biggest strength, namely, its integrated in-house development and manufacturing of everything from EV batteries to the EV itself. Unlike other domestic competitors, BYD had roots in vertical integration since its inception. This is because Wang recognized that China's greatest advantage was labor cost, which led to the idea that making everything in-house is cost-efficient and more reliable than buying from others (Liu 2007). In the early days when competing with Sanyo and other multinational giants, Wang used manual labor, instead of automation. When producing automobiles, he used the same principle. He once visited an automobile mold factory in Japan and saw engineers lying down on the production line to polish the mold, and he noted, "If our engineers did the same work, China would have a cost advantage" (Liu 2007).

Three years after purchasing Xi'an Qinchuan, in 2006, BYD created its first pure electric sedan, the F3e, equipped with its self-developed iron-phosphate battery. However, because of the uncertainty of the national policy and the lack of charging facilities, BYD gave up commercialization and pivoted its focus to hybrid technology. In 2008, the year that Tesla launched its Roadster, BYD launched its first NEV and the world's first mass-produced PHEV. The market success of the F3, which has a gasoline engine, and the introduction of a PHEV persuaded Warren Buffett to invest $230 million in BYD in 2008.

In 2009, BYD's car sales surpassed Chery's (an ICE automobile producer) for the first time, and BYD became the largest independent automobile manufacturer in China. That same year, the General Office of the State Council issued the "Automobile Industry Adjustment and Revitalization Plan," which for the first time supported the development of NEVs at the national level and introduced subsidy policies for NEVs. In 2009, BYD acquired the Hunan Midea Bus Manufacturing Co. and gained manufacturing capacity that could be used for electric buses.

Also in 2009, the Shenzhen Municipal People's Government issued the "Notice on the Issuance of Shenzhen New Energy Industry Revitalization and Development Policies." Wang quickly recognized this as an institutional opportunity and heralded BYD's "electrification of public transportation" strategy, with the goal of replacing city buses and taxis with electric versions. In 2010, the Shenzhen government proposed an initiative to adopt BYD's electric taxis and buses, so Shenzhen became the first city in China to promote EVs in public transportation.

BYD gradually increased the percentage of EVs in production since 2017 and completely stopped producing ICE vehicles in March 2022. In 2024, BYD realized a profit of approximately RMB 40 billion and sold an annual total of 4.27 million vehicles. In 2023, BYD was the second-largest seller of BEVs and sold the most PHEVs in the world. The turning point came in the fourth quarter of 2024, when BYD topped the BEV sales chart for the first time. But BYD's most impressive achievements were based in the Chinese market. A market of 1.4 billion people, a forward-looking industrial policy, and a rapidly rising group of industrious engineer-entrepreneurs were all important reasons for BYD's success.

3.2.2 NIO

In contrast to BYD, NIO is representative of the new stream of "internet car" companies. NIO was founded in November 2014 by Li Bin, who had previously founded two successful internet companies. As a member of a new generation of entrepreneurs in the mobile internet era, Li believed that building an innovation-centric business model was more important than becoming a traditional car company. As he said in an interview, "consumers buy electric cars because of a better experience. A better user experience while protecting the environment is what all consumers want" (Yu 2016).

Unlike traditional car manufacturers that started by developing products and establishing sales networks, NIO started in an unconventional way by forming the FE Formula E racing team to compete in FIA competitions. At the Hong Kong round of the Formula E Championship, Li announced the initial details about the company's first concept car, the EP9. Further, Li chose London as the location for the launch of this supercar. Only six of these fully electric supercars, which had performance comparable to Ferrari with a maximum of up to 1,000 horsepower and acceleration from 0 to 100 km/h in less than three second, were built. The buyers of the six available vehicles were all investors in NIO, including Pony Ma, founder of Tencent; Lei Jun, founder of Xiaomi; and Richard Liu, founder of Jingdong. The media announcement was clearly intended to attract public attention and establish a high-end image.

The company's core management team consists of senior automobile executives, including former executives from Tesla, BMW, Volkswagen, General Motors, the GAC Group, and other well-known domestic and international companies. NIO's current president, Qin Lihong, was previously the deputy general manager of Chery Automobile Sales Company and has more than ten years of experience in brand communications and marketing in the auto market. Shen Feng, the executive vice president, was previously the president of Volvo's EV brand in China, Polestar.

In April 2017, NIO launched its first production model, the ES8, targeting the mid- to high-end market with a price ranging from RMB 448,000 to RMB 548,000. Production was handled by the JAC Automobile Group. In 2018, sales of the ES8 totaled 11,348 vehicles, surpassing those of the Tesla Model X in China (9,413). In June 2019, NIO launched its second production model, the ES6, intended to compete with Tesla's Model 3. On September 12, 2018, NIO was listed on the New York Stock Exchange (NYSE), becoming the world's second EV company listed on the US stock exchange since 2010, when Tesla was listed (see Table 1).

Table 1 Major events in NIO's history

Time	Representative events
November 25, 2014	NIO founded in Shanghai
June 1, 2015	Won FIA Formula E Championship
August 1, 2015	NIO UK launched
September 1, 2015	NIO North America launched
April 6, 2016	Strategic cooperation agreement with JAC
April 28, 2016	Construction of electric motor production base in Nanjing
November 21, 2016	English brand name NIO and the electric sports car "EP9" unveiled in London
March 10, 2017	First concept car, EVE was released
April 19, 2017	First debut in Shanghai Motor Show
May 18, 2017	NIO energy project launched in Wuhan
September 12, 2018	Listed on New York Stock Exchange
December 2018	ES6 launched
May 28, 2019	Strategic agreement with Beijing Yizhuang State Investment
February 25, 2020	Chinese headquarter officially opened in Hefei
July 24, 2020	SUV EC6 launched
January 9, 2021	First sedan model "the ET7" launched
October, 2021	NIO Center opened in Norway
January, 2022	Strategic partnership with Baosteel Group
March 10, 2022	Listed on the Hong Kong Stock Exchange
September 29, 2022	NIO battery exchange station built in Germany
October 18, 2022	Vehicle deliveries began in Germany, the Netherlands, Denmark, and Sweden.
October 21, 2022	NIO Battery Technology established in Hefei
December 1, 2022	Battery exchange station opened in the Netherlands
December 17, 2022	NIO Center opened in Berlin
February 1, 2023	The electric SUV "Azerra EL7" released in Europe.
March 6, 2023	Exchange station opened in Denmark

According to the company's sales data, NIO's sales for January–September 2023 totaled less than 110,000 vehicles, far below the target proposed by Li Bin in 2022 of 245,000. Bloomberg also reported that, in the face of fierce competition, NIO suffered an annual loss in 2023 (Bloomberg 2024). The situation starts to improve in 2024, as the scale and profitability of after-sales services continue to grow. The latest sales data show that the company has finally ushered in positive growth, with a total of 221,970 new cars delivered in 2024, an increase of 38.7 percent over the previous year.

3.2.3 CATL

In 1989, Zeng Yujun, who had received a bachelor's degree in oceanic engineering from Shanghai Jiaotong University, joined Dongguan Shinko Electronics (SAE), a company jointly established with the TDK Corporation in Japan, which was the world's largest manufacturer of computer hard disk heads at the time. He started his career as an engineer and eventually became the only mainland Chinese senior manager. While at SAE, he earned a master's degree in electronic information engineering from the South China University of Technology and a PhD in condensed matter physics from the Chinese Academy of Sciences.

At SAE, Zeng met several people who played an important role in the subsequent birth of Contemporary Amperex Technology (CATL). In 1994, Zhang Yujie, who had graduated from National Taiwan University and then received a PhD from the University of Notre Dame in 1973, joined SAE. Previously, he had worked at the Ford Motor Company and IBM in the United States. Zhang became Zeng's supervisor.

Another key person was Liang Shaokang, a graduate of Hong Kong University, who became the CEO of SAE in 1999 and was Zeng's direct boss. As early as 1997 when MP3s had just appeared and there was a growing demand for small, high-energy batteries, Liang recognized the huge market potential for batteries in consumer electronics. He then proposed that TDK expand to the production of lithium batteries, however, TDK rejected this idea. As a result, Liang encouraged a group of executives to spin off and start their own business. In 1999, Liang, Zhang, and Zeng, as well as several others, resigned and started Amperex Technology Limited (ATL) in Hong Kong. This new company focused on research, development, production, and sales of lithium-ion batteries.

In 2002, ATL became a battery supplier for the Apple iPod. Despite this initial success, in 2005, due to increased market competition, investors sold their shares in ATL, which was acquired by TDK for $100 million. As a result, ATL went from being a Chinese company to being owned by a Japanese firm.

In 2008, ATL established a Power Battery Department to develop car batteries. This was fortuitous, as shortly thereafter, the Chinese government announced industrial policies to promote the development of NEVs. Then, in 2011, in order to protect China's NEV enterprises and lithium battery industry, which were still relatively weak, the government introduced the "Guidance Catalog for Foreign Investment Industries"; this explicitly restricted the production of car batteries by wholly foreign-owned enterprises, preventing ATL from making car batteries for the Chinese market.

In response, Zeng unsuccessfully proposed separating production of ATL's car battery from TDK. Then, Zeng and the rest of the board of directors formed a new firm in Ningde (Zeng's hometown in Fujian Province) and established CATL. In 2012, the Chinese government released the "Energy-saving and New Energy Vehicle Industry Plan (2012–2020)," which proposed that, by 2015, power battery modules should achieve energy density of more than 150Wh/kg, a goal that, at that time, only lithium batteries had attained. BYD, the other domestic market leader, was vertically integrated (it sold BYD batteries only for BYD cars), thereby leaving a large unmet market for CATL. In 2016, BYD was the largest domestic battery producer, but, already by 2017, CATL's power battery sales reached 12 GWh, surpassing BYD's 7.2 GWh – and as a result CATL became the world's top automotive battery producer.

3.3 Other Chinese EV Startups

3.3.1 Xpeng

In June 2014, Xia Heng and He Tao as well as more than ten others at GAC Research Institute founded Xpeng Auto. At almost the same time, He Xiaopeng's browser application company UC merged with Alibaba, a deal worth nearly $4 billion, making it the largest merger and acquisition investment in China's internet industry. He Xiaopeng joined Alibaba as the president of Alibaba Mobile Business Group, the chairman of Ali Games, and the president of Tudou.com.

In August 2014, He Xiaopeng began to incubate Xpeng Auto as an investor. The staff of the company grew to more than 50 in mid-2015. More than 90 percent of Xpeng Auto employees were technical staff, who had mainly come from well-known auto companies such as GAC, BMW, Ford, and Peugeot Citroën, large auto parts companies such as Delphi, and technology/IT companies such as Samsung, Huawei, and Tencent. He

Table 2 Major Events in Xpeng's History

Time	Representative events
2014	Co-founded in Guangzhou
September 23, 2016	All-electric BETA SUV launched
May 4, 2017	Factory opened in Zhaoqing
August 29, 2017	He Xiaopeng joined Xpeng as chairman
October 12, 2017	First mass production model launched
December 15, 2017	Alibaba invested in Xpeng
January 10, 2018	World debut at CES (International Consumer Electronics Show)
March 7, 2018	First supercharging station completed in Guangzhou
December 12, 2018	First production model (G3) launched and delivered
June 2019	10,000 vehicles delivered
April 27, 2020	P7 launched with a maximum range of 706 km
September 24, 2020	G3i exported to Norway
April 8, 2021	Construction of Manufacturing Base and R&D Center
July 7, 2021	Listed on the Hong Kong Stock Exchange
February 10, 2022	Agreement with Swedish dealer Bilia for new car sales
March 11, 2022	Pre-order sales of P5 in Denmark, the Netherlands, Norway, and Sweden
January, 2023	Service centers opened in Norway, the Netherlands, Sweden and Denmark
February 20, 2023	Guangzhou plant begins operations with annual production capacity of 120,000 units
March 26, 2023	New mid-size sedan P7i began delivery

Xiaopeng left Alibaba on August 22, 2017, and joined Xpeng Auto as the chairman on August 29.

In December 2018, Xpeng launched its first mass-production model, the G3 (with a range of 350 kilometers), in partnership with Zhengzhou Haima Automobile. The G3 quickly gained popularity with the younger generation because of the high-tech style of its body and features such as voice recognition and automatic parking. On August 27, 2020, the company was listed on the NYSE (see Table 2).

3.3.2 Li Auto

In July 2015, Li Xiang, who had started Auto House and Bubble.com, founded Li Auto, with the goal of making it a luxury intelligent EV brand. Li recruited R&D staff with industry experience from major domestic ICE

Table 3 Major events in Li Auto's history

Time	Representative events
July 1, 2015	Li Xiang founded Li Auto
October 18, 2018	Launch of the first model, Ideal ONE
November 20, 2019	Mass production of Ideal ONE
July 30, 2020	listed on NASDAQ
December 4, 2019	Achieved a record of delivering 30,000 vehicles in 12 months
April 2021	More than 50,000 Ideal ONEs delivered
July 10, 2021	Opened 100th directly operated retail center
August 12, 2021	Listed on the Hong Kong Stock Exchange
October 2021	Opened Beijing Green Intelligent Factory
October 28, 2021	100,000th Ideal ONE rolled off the production line

joint ventures and independent manufacturers. In October 2018, Li Auto launched its first product, Ideal ONE, priced at RMB 320,000; deliveries began in December 2019, with sales of 1,000 vehicles in 2019, 32,600 in 2020, and 90,491 in 2021, achieving rapid sales growth with a single model. On July 30, 2020, the company went public on the NASDAQ. The following year in 2021, Li Auto was listed on the Stock Exchange of Hong Kong (see Table 3).

The year 2023 was extremely important for Li Auto. Whereas most EV startups (e.g., NIO and Xpeng) struggled with annual losses, Li Auto's sales exceeded 370,000 vehicles, enabling it to become profitable for the first time since its founding, with net profit totaling RMB 11.81 billion.

3.3.3 Hozon Auto

Hozon was founded in 2014 in Zhejiang Province. Neta is the company's EV brand. Based on EV sales in the Chinese market, Hozon was in fourth place in 2021, behind Xpeng, Li Auto, and NIO. While its rivals competed in the high-end EV market, Hozon focused on the low-cost market. Its first product, the Nezha N01, a small SUV, was launched in November 2018 at the low price of RMB 66,800–76,800. In 2022, Neta had record sales, 150,000 vehicles, and was in first place in domestic sales, but failed to reach its sales target of 250,000 vehicles in 2023 due to fierce competition from other domestic competitors. In August 2022, Hozon began to export to Southeast Asia (see Table 4).

Table 4 Major events in Hozon Auto's history

Time	Representative events
October 2014	Established in Tongxiang, Zhejiang Province
June 2018	Production license for NEVs issued by the Ministry of Industry and Information Technology
July 2018	Nezha NO1 rolled off the production line
November 2018	First debut at the Guangzhou Motor Show
March 2020	"Nezha U" launched
November 2020	"Nezha V" launched
October 2021	Obtained 4 billion RMB in funding
November 2021	Announcement of strategic alliance with CATL
August 2022	Exports to Southeast Asia (Thailand)
March 10, 2023	Construction of the first overseas factory in Thailand

3.3.4 Leap Motor

Leap Motor was founded in Hangzhou, Zhejiang Province, in 2015. In an interview, its founder, Zhu Jiangming, claimed that he had known nothing about car manufacturing: "In 2015, when we first decided to build a car, we didn't know what kind of expertise we had in cars, and we really had no idea who to hire" (Wang 2022). He once told the media that, among the company's 400-plus employees, 80 percent were R&D staff, but the core team had no prior experience in the automotive industry (Sohu 2017). Like many other startup EV companies, the company also had difficulty obtaining a production certification license. Not until December 2020 did it acquire a small local car company and obtain the permission to produce EVs.

On September 29, 2022, Leap Motor was listed on the Hong Kong stock market, and it became the fourth startup to be listed on the capital market, following NIO, Xpeng, and Li Auto. In 2023, the company sold a total of 144,000 vehicles, but had a net loss of RMB 4.216 billion. On May 14, 2024, Stellantis and Leap Motor announced the establishment of Leap Motor International, a joint venture between the two companies based in Amsterdam (see Table 5).

3.4 Startups by Other Chinese Technology Firms

The booming Chinese EV market attracted new entrants from adjacent industries. One landmark event was the launch of the SU7 EV sedan by Xiaomi, a well-known Chinese smartphone and consumer electronics giant, on March 2024, nearly three years after it had announced it was joining the EV industry. Founded

Table 5 Major events in Leap Motor's history

Time	Representative events
December 24, 2015	Leap Motor established
November 2017	First production model S01 launched
December 2017	Obtained pre-A round of funding from Sequoia China
June 2018	Strategic alliance with Dahua to develop AI self-driving chip
October 2018	S01s rolled off the production line
November 2018	Opened the first directly operated retail store
April 2019	First crossover pure electric SUV model "C-more" launched
May 2019	Obtained the license for on-road testing of intelligent connected vehicles
August 2019	Obtained 360 million RMB in financing
May 9, 2020	Strategic agreement with FAW Group
November 2020	Debut at Guangzhou Motor Show
January 2021	Strategic cooperation agreement with Hefei Municipal Government
January 2021	Obtained 4.3 billion RMB in financing
August 10, 2021	Completed a new round of financing totaling 4.5 billion RMB
September 28, 2021	Leap Motor C11 launched
June 28, 2022	100,000th C11 rolled off the production line.
September 29, 2022	Listed on the Hong Kong Stock Exchange.
September 30, 2022	Strategic cooperation agreement with Faurecia
November 22, 2022	Opened overseas stores in Israel
February 1, 2023	165,100 vehicles delivered in total

in 2010, Xiaomi sold products with performance comparable to the iPhone but at lower prices. Although early on, the company was described as an "Apple copycat," after a long evolution, it expanded from selling smartphones to offering Internet of Things (IoT) applications as well as lifestyle and internet services. The company's internet services include advertising, paid apps, and games. Xiaomi offers an even richer lineup of IoT devices than Apple, including not only smartphones and tablets but also TV-sets, smartwatches, vacuum cleaner robots, and smart home appliances – inspiring legions of *mifan*, that is, enthusiastic fans of its products.

Lei Jun, Xiaomi's founder and CEO, shocked the world in 2021, when he announced plans for his company to expand its core business into EVs. Xiaomi offers three versions of the SU7; the standard version has a starting range of 700 kilometers (435 miles), which is farther than that of the long-range version of the Tesla Model 3. The selling point of the SU7 is that it combines Xiaomi's core competence in software with intelligent features, such as an autonomous driving system and a digital cockpit, making it a unique EV made by a tech giant. It also lowered its costs by using a "Gigacast," in which the car body is molded entirely from aluminum alloy. After its debut on March 28, 2004, the presales of the SU7 totaled 50,000 vehicles in just 27 minutes, and 88,898 were reserved within 24 hours. The Xiaomi SU7 sparked a fierce price war in the already crowded Chinese EV market.

3.5 Other Actors in the Chinese EV Industry

China's major state-owned automobile manufacturers had a historical path of manufacturing ICE vehicles based on foreign technology through joint ventures with foreign ICE legacy automobile manufacturers. Large state-owned Chinese manufacturers face the same challenges as all other global ICE manufacturers in terms of their path-dependent commitment to ICE cars. Unsurprisingly, the Chinese large incumbent automobile manufacturers faced sharp competition from domestic automakers (e.g., BYD) as well as pressure from the central or local government to facilitate the transition to EVs.

As a result, the incumbent automakers announced plans and timetables for electrification. Although they still manufacture ICE vehicles, they also shifted to increasing their share of the EV market by launching new brands and adjusting the product mix. For example, SAIC invested in and developed four EV brands targeting different markets; IM is a joint venture among SAIC Motor, Zhangjiang Hi-Tech Park, and Alibaba Group and is positioned as the group's premium EV brand; and Roewe and Fefan are aimed at local Chinese consumers. SAIC is enhancing its global presence by strengthening its MG brand, which it acquired in the UK.

3.6 Conclusion

The rapid growth in China's EV industry and the emergence of startups is a stunning historical counterexample to the "productivity dilemma" that has plagued the automobile industry for decades (Abernathy 1978). The combination of Tesla and the Chinese entrants has meant that the ICE-based technology paradigm and its long-term dominant design are being disrupted and overwhelmed by the startups that have emerged in China and leading the historical transition to EVs.

As described in this section, most of these EV startups did not come from the automobile industry. BYD was originally a battery company, and NIO did not even have a license to produce cars. This bottom up entrepreneurial activity was possible, not only because of government subsidies, but also by the fact that compared to ICE vehicles, EVs are simpler, with fewer components; therefore, their development had lower barriers to entry and costs for entrepreneurs. Another basis for the steady stream of new entrants was the rapid build-out of EV-centric supply chain, in which a large number of local component suppliers provided key components, such as batteries, thus facilitating entry into the EV industry in a way that was unprecedented.

China's EV manufacturers emerged and have grown rapidly, benefiting greatly from the testing ground enabled by the government's initial support and the huge domestic market. The EU and the United States are erecting trade barriers to exclude Chinese EV manufacturers from their domestic markets. However, the multipronged technological advances of Chinese EV and battery producers are putting significant pressure on all existing ICE-based incumbents, as well as others, including Tesla. Chinese EV producers appear certain to lead the global EV market, and the technological transition to electrification appears to be progressing on "China speed."

Chinese success in the EV industry was the outcome of its NEV policy that was initially vague but became increasingly concrete as domestic entrepreneurs built and marketed vehicles. The government monitored the market and repeatedly intervened through the use of various incentives and subsidies to address bottlenecks and market inefficiencies in the supply chain, consumer adoption, and R&D, as well as addressing problems such as corruption. Chinese EV manufacturers succeeded in not only introducing but also dominating in sales to the point that foreign joint ventures with the state-owned automakers also began to reorient their operations to focus on exporting EVs to third markets or even their home markets. China's model of evolving government policy and entrepreneurial action has enabled the country to become the center of not just global EV production but R&D and innovation. Its centrality is reinforced by the fact that Tesla, now the best-known EV manufacturer, has its largest factory there, and its largest competitors, such as BYD, NIO, and Xpeng, are Chinese.

4 Emergence of the EV Supplier Ecosystem in China

By definition, a social and technical transition from a core general-purpose technology, such as the internal combustion engine (ICE), requires creating a new supply chain, but also a new way of thinking. In this case, that transition is from a system based on petroleum to one based on batteries, which probably –

but not necessarily – will be made with lithium. While car batteries have existed for a long time, for years, they were heavy lead acid batteries, used mainly in ignition systems. Over time, batteries have evolved dramatically. The greatest change was the replacement of earlier vehicle battery chemical compositions by lithium – a technology that was initially used in portable electronic devices. And yet, the dominant design in terms of battery storage material is still subject to some uncertainty.

If China wished to play a leading role in the EV transition, it would have to build an entire ecosystem more or less simultaneously. Many of the components of the new ecosystem – such as an electricity grid, auto bodies, tires, and brakes – already existed, and so did manufacturers that could join the emerging social and EV technical ecosystem. Similarly, China did have various battery makers, especially, for portable devices, though their technology was not yet cutting-edge. Hence, many parts of what would become the new ecosystem already existed in China and elsewhere; however, the ICE system was entrenched, and many other capabilities would have to be developed to support the emerging EV system.

Because EVs represent a disruptive technology, there was space for EV startup entrants to displace traditional ICE manufacturers that were caught between protecting their existing ICE businesses and entering the initially uncertain new industry. This dramatic technological disruption threatened not only the skills and knowledge base of the traditional manufacturers but also the capabilities of much of their supplier base, that is, essentially all the skills related to internal combustion – including engines, fuel, ignition, and exhaust systems – affecting products from gas tanks and spark plugs to catalytic converters and mufflers. Few firms involved in producing parts for ICE vehicles are expected to survive in the EV age, absent their own transition. Other firms, such as those involved in the business of tires, windshields, brakes, and auto body parts, should be able to survive the transition. But, in some activities, such as tires and brake manufacturing, global leaders will have to reengineer their products to be optimized for EVs – for example, brakes that generate electricity or tires built for the different torque and wear characteristics of an EV (Hankook 2024).

In this section, we examine how China created the world's most comprehensive EV supply chain and the remarkable rise of Chinese suppliers, particularly in batteries. As late as 2017, Japanese and Korean automotive battery suppliers were dominant globally (Yeung 2019), only to be displaced in the 2020s. Moreover, a number of non-Chinese suppliers began to move significant EV-related engineering capability to China – thereby reinforcing it as the global center of EVs.[39] Moreover, China is quickly becoming the location for global technological leaders in nearly every aspect of the battery supply chain. This development challenges the competitive position of auto assemblers in the European Union (EU) and the United States, which will increasingly depend on imported parts from China or risk producing obsolete or excessively expensive vehicles.[40] Finally, we reflect on the implications of components developed for EVs, such as batteries, for other industries, such as energy storage for utilities or innovations in electrical motors for cars that might be useful for those used in factories.

The greater simplicity of EV technology and manufacturing requirements is likely to reduce the number of suppliers, as EVs require far fewer parts than ICE-powered vehicles. Even as the number of EV components is fewer, the production of many of these remaining components will require capabilities that are entirely different from those needed for ICE. The drivetrain technologies will also shift and new configurations become possible such as equipping each wheel with an electrical motor, rather than having only one central motor – something that was nearly impossible in ICE-powered vehicles.

Despite the rapid progress, it appears as though battery technology is still at an early point in its scientific, engineering, and manufacturing evolution. Nevertheless, the existing lithium-based batteries are currently widely installed, and highly automated manufacturing processes are operating at the latest battery giga-factories in China, Korea, and the United States.

The growth and strength of the EV supplier ecosystem demonstrates Chinese competitiveness based on the speed and comprehensiveness of the ecosystem's formation and maturation. This growth was due to both government policy and entrepreneurial activity. At this point in the evolution of EVs, the technological ferment in batteries appears to be central for continuing progress of the entire system. For assemblers, the make-or-buy decision seems to be central – firms producing ICE vehicles combined engine production and final assembly. No dominant organizational design has emerged yet in the EV industry – for instance, BYD has combined battery production and auto assembly while also selling batteries to other assemblers. Similarly, Tesla produces its own batteries and purchases batteries from others. Finally, CATL and other battery producers supply batteries to assemblers. Auto assemblers that purchase batteries no

---

[39] For example, Bosch (2024), the giant German auto parts maker, specifically mentions electrified mobility as one specialization of its Shanghai research center. The only other Bosch research center that identifies EVs as an area of research is the main laboratory in Germany.

[40] This is certain to be a conundrum, as the United States attempts to protect its market with local content regulations, while effectively banning Chinese firms from producing in the United States. Japanese automakers were allowed to establish factories in the United States, thereby internalizing their production in North America (see, e.g., Kenney & Florida 1993). It reads fine.

longer make the highest value-added component of an automobile (the engine). For incumbent assemblers that use an Internal Combustion Engine as a major product differentiator, relying on new outside vendors for the electric battery (the major product differentiator) is very likely to be viewed as a competitive liability.

Finally, the Chinese EV ecosystem threatens to become so advanced that it will make the rest of world dependent on it. For example, Tesla's Shanghai factory is already its lowest-cost location, and German automakers are importing Chinese-made EVs to Europe. The strength of Chinese ecosystem may make it increasingly difficult for other countries, such as the United States and EU member countries, to impose sanctions on Chinese EVs and batteries, as this could be a choice to remain technological and economic laggards with higher cost structures than China.[41]

4.1 Chinese Government Policy for Suppliers

The Chinese firm decisions to pursue EVs were a gradual and evolving process that was encouraged and incentivized by various government initiatives at the national and local levels. Government policy was informed and supported by external developments, such as continuing global adoption of hybrids, advancing general Chinese R&D capacity, advances in battery technology in China and globally, and rapid growth in the Chinese ICE auto market and industry. Recognizing and trying to shape these changes, the government's plans were directed not only at the assembler level but at also the ability to access raw materials and manufacture key components (IEA 2022a).

Only ten years earlier, the Chinese government had not yet chosen the winning technology but, rather, was incentivizing experimentation in EVs as well as fuel cells and more efficient ICE. This drive to develop alternative energy vehicles began in the Tenth FYP, focusing on key components, such as batteries and drive trains, but, at the time, most of the attention was on R&D at universities and automakers that were state-owned enterprises (SOEs) (Lu et al. 2014). For example, in 2001, in the Tenth FYP, the Ministry of Science and Technology launched the Major Science and Technology Special Project for Electric Vehicles under the 863 Plan, concentrating on the three verticals (hybrid vehicles, pure electric vehicles, and fuel cell vehicles) and the three horizontals (i.e., powertrain control system, the electric drive motor and control system, and the power storage battery system) (Gong & Hansen 2023). In this

---

[41] To illustrate, in late 2024 Europe's hopes for building an independent battery industry was shaken by the bankruptcy of the Swedish battery startup, Northvolt, after expending over $15 billion in government funding and venture capital.

early period, the activities regarding components consisted largely of research and knowledge development, not the development of actual supply chain capacity.

The Chinese government has also supported R&D in all significant nodes of the EV supply chain. The process of developing capability continued in 2012, as the State Council issued a plan for the promotion "of large-scale production of power batteries, accelerate the cultivation and development of a group of power battery production enterprises with continuous innovation capabilities, and strive to form 2–3 leading enterprises [and] 2–3 backbone production enterprises in key material fields." The plan specifically mentions the components to be developed: "positive and negative electrodes, separators, and electrolytes of power batteries and their production, control and testing equipment, and develop new super capacitors and their combined systems with batteries" (State Council 2012). It reiterates the need for the government to increase understanding of the requirements for building a complete supply chain and a techno-economic regime similar to the one in the ICE auto industry, which mostly consisted of joint ventures between Chinese SOEs and foreign automakers (which, as mentioned earlier, were intent on avoiding the transfer of technology to China).

The Chinese government also introduced local content regulations for suppliers.[42] In March 2015, the Ministry of Industry and Information Technology issued "Specification Conditions for Automobile and Energy Storage Battery Industry," and whitelisted companies in the industry that met them. EV original equipment manufacturers (OEMs) that wanted to receive government subsidies could only use batteries produced by companies on the whitelist – all of which were Chinese companies. Having received national support as they prepared for the EV revolution, China's battery companies were granted a window for developing and rapidly increasing their global market share.

Chinese banks (which are SOEs) provided the funding for building the supply chain in the form of loans to Chinese firms that sought ownership in mining and processing facilities in foreign countries (Graham et al. 2021: 73). Many of the firms thus funded are either integrated with or have relational contracts with key suppliers.

Chinese government policy has used a wide variety of policy instruments to develop a complete EV supplier ecosystem. Next, we outline the dimensions of this ecosystem.

---

[42] The United States is introducing extremely stringent local content regulations for BEVs to be sold in the United States in order to force foreign firms to build factories in the United States, even as it is preventing Chinese battery producers from producing there.

4.2 Developing a Supplier Ecosystem

The rapid growth in the Chinese EV industry created enormous demand for components and materials such as lithium and graphite as the main materials in EV batteries, which are very different from those in ICE vehicles.[43] China dominates production at every stage of the EV battery supply chain beginning with control of 80 percent of Lithium mines. In heavy industry, SOEs were important investors in building mines around the world, particularly for lithium. However, component suppliers are often either existing firms extending their product lines (e.g., graphite producers) or new entrants. Supplier production was highly concentrated in a few firms globally, and, just as important, Chinese producers have become even more important since 2021 (IEA 2022b).

Table 6 gives a partial list of the main Chinese suppliers of EV inputs. In 2024, nearly three-quarters of the battery cell, specialized cathode, and anode material production capacity is in China. Also, China has 70 percent of the global cathode and 85 percent of anode material production capacity and over half the global raw material processing of lithium, cobalt, and graphite. China dominates the entire graphite anode supply chain end to end, as it has 80 percent of the global graphite mining (IEA 2022b: 29).

4.2.1 Batteries

Figure 5 shows that the majority of EV production costs are due to Li-ion batteries. Because of the centrality of the battery in an EV, this section is necessarily short. In less than a decade, China went from being relatively backward and an unimportant actor in the vehicle battery industry to the global leader in production, though China continues to lag behind its Asian competitors in patenting (Gong & Hansen 2023). The two main Chinese battery firms are CATL and BYD (which, along with Tesla, is now the largest EV producer in the world). The Chinese firms became leaders partly because of their shift in battery materials (e.g., Prius used nickel manganese cobalt) to lithium-iron-phosphate (LFP) and, perhaps later, to sodium (see Figure 6).

4.2.2 Electric Motors

In 2023, EV motors were produced in-house by OEMs or purchased from various suppliers. For example, BYD produces not only its own batteries but also electric motors. Although not many EV assemblers appear to have done

---

[43] ICE vehicles use iron and aluminum in engines and various other components, such as exhaust manifolds, and platinum for catalytic converters and so forth. In contrast, BEVs require lithium for batteries and many rare earths. Of course, if sodium replaces lithium, supply chains would change once again.

Table 6 Key Chinese component suppliers

Chinese supplier	Input	Global market share (if available)
Zhuhai Enjie New Material Technology	Separator membranes	n/a
Shanghai Putailai New Energy Technology	Separator membranes	n/a
Jiangxi Tinci Central Advanced Materials	Electrolyte salts	35%
Zhangjiagang Guotai-Huarong New Chemical Materials	Electrolyte salts	n/a
Shenzhen Capchem Technology	Electrolyte salts	n/a
Ningbo Shanshan	Electrolyte salts	n/a
Ningbo Shanshan	Anode material (graphite)	50%
Shanghai Putailai New Energy Technology	Anode material (graphite)	50%
BTR New Energy Materials	Anode material (graphite)	50%
Chinese suppliers	Manganese sulfate	~90%
Chinese miners	Natural graphite mining	80%
Chinese recyclers	Recycling	~50%

Source: Author compilation based on IEA (2022b).

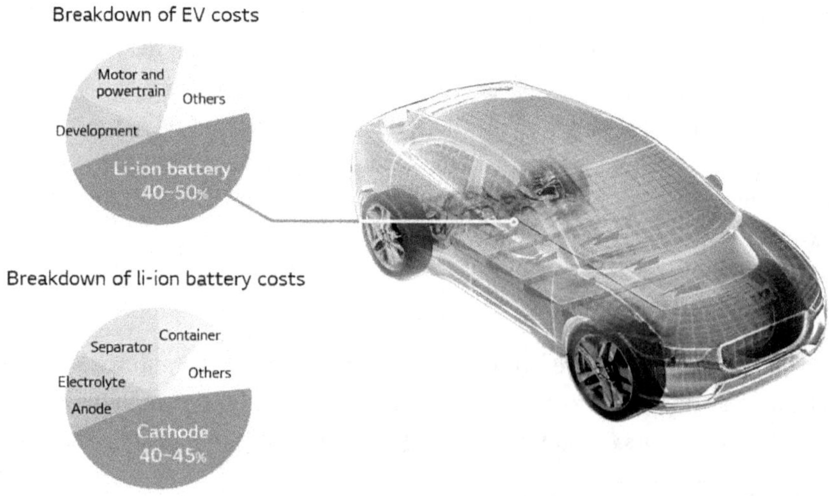

Figure 5 EV cost structure 2022

Source: www.foreverev.com/2022/12/ev-li-ion-battery-cost-structure/

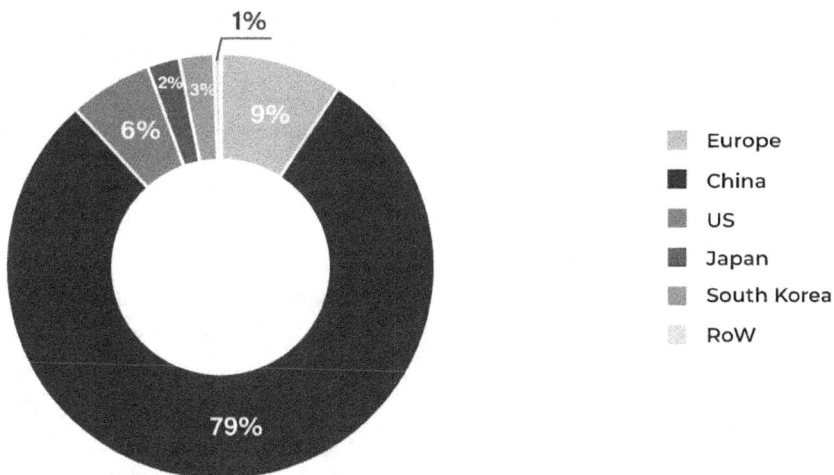

Figure 6 EV battery manufacturing capacity, by region
Source: www.precedenceresearch.com/insights/electric-vehicle-battery-market

the same, according to a McKinsey (2023) report, those that make more than 100,000 vehicles per year are expected to move powertrain production in-house. Many EV powertrain producers are operating in 2024, including non-Chinese Tier One automobile parts suppliers, such as Bosch, Denso, Magna, and Valeo, and several startups. Chinese assemblers and various parts suppliers (including battery firms, such as CATL) produce EV motors. However, R&D in the battery space has intensified globally and new battery designs are frequently highlighted in industry related publications.

Foreign EV drivetrain manufacturers, including major European OEMs and Tesla, have invested in both production and R&D operations in China. For example, in 2017, Magna, a giant premier Canadian automotive supplier, established a joint venture with Huayu Automotive Systems to support Magna's first e-drivetrain business in China, which is intended to supply a German automaker (Magna 2017). Similarly, Punch Powertrain, a Belgian company purchased by the Chinese Yinyi Group, built significant production capacity and R&D facilities in China for the development of EV drivetrains.[44]

China has become the center of electric motor R&D, because of the size and diversity of the Chinese market for electric motors to power not only automobiles but also all kinds of vehicles, from buses to bicycles. It is not

---

[44] When Yinyi, a real estate group, had financial problems, it was purchased by a consortium of Chinese firms consisting of Fosun, Geely, and Haier.

yet clear whether, in the long term, a large independent electric motor industry will exist or the industry will be absorbed by auto assemblers or battery producers, such as CATL or BYD, which have battery expertise and might be able to optimize the relationship between battery packs and electric motors.

4.2.3 Semiconductors

EVs use more and more sophisticated semiconductors than traditional ICE vehicles (Deloitte, 2021). Although these semiconductors are not extremely sophisticated compared to those in computers and smartphones, they have been largely designed and produced by US and European manufacturers. Because of increasing trade tensions between the United States/Europe and China and the volume of Chinese EV production and their importance in the Chinese economy, it is not surprising that China has begun to implement policies for replacing foreign semiconductors with Chinese products.[45] EVs use a large number of semiconductors, so this is an enormous market, in which, as mentioned earlier, the incumbent (foreign) ICE-related semiconductor firms might not have a powerful historical advantage.

4.2.4 Infrastructure: Charging Stations

The transition to EVs obviously requires the construction of charging infrastructure. In contrast to the available infrastructure necessary for the adoption of ICE vehicles more than a century earlier, most of the infrastructure for charging EVs already exists, in the sense of an electrical grid for distributing electricity. Thus, the final node, the charging station, had to be built. Very early on, the Chinese government recognized the need for this infrastructure and charged local governments with installing it in 2015.[46] As a result, by 2025 China had installed over 60 percent of the global EV charging stations. But, more important, China had 90 percent of the fast chargers and an installed base of 760,000, compared with 70,000 in Europe (IEA 2023). As a result, "range anxiety" is far less problematic in China than in the United States or the EU, as it has so many charging locations.

The economics of infrastructure are different for EVs than for ICE vehicles, in the sense that fuel for ICE vehicles could be accessed only at gas stations that were eventually built in large numbers across the country to ensure that fuel would be widely available. Moreover, ICE vehicles required an entire

---

[45] https://economictimes.indiatimes.com/news/international/business/buy-local-chips-china-urges-ev-makers-as-us-clash-deepens/articleshow/108532932.cms?from=mdr/.
[46] www.gov.cn/zhengce/zhengceku/2015-10/09/content_10214.htm.

supply chain, from oil drilling and refining to delivery to the end user. The transition to EVs presented fewer complex issues than the adoption of ICE vehicles, as the electrical grid had already been built, that is, the problem of energy delivery was already solved. Not only was it necessary to have charging stations at home, but public charging stations also needed to be built – a nontrivial task as can be seen by the shortage of public charging stations in the United States.[47] Thus, developing the infrastructure presents different issues because demand will be lower for recharging stations than for gas stations, as most EVs can be charged at home, thereby changing the economics of "refueling." Also, the increasing range of newer EVs decreases demand for charging away from home.

China has built the world's largest network of charging infrastructure, and Chinese firms are also beginning to build the charging infrastructure in other countries, such as Mexico and countries in Southeast Asia.[48] The sheer volume of Chinese charging infrastructure production suggests that these firms will also be able to improve charging times and lower costs due to economies of scale. This might enable Chinese firms to increase exports of infrastructure as well and compete with European and US producers (Cao 2024).

4.2.5 CATL Supply Chain

BYD, which began as a battery producer and also supplies batteries to other auto assemblers, largely integrated the supply chain. CATL, the world's largest battery producer, developed its own supply chain and supplies an increasing number of auto assemblers, including Tesla, Toyota, BMW, and myriad Chinese assemblers. Finally, it also built battery factories around the world (see Table 7).

As the largest battery producer in the world, CATL has developed its own supply chain. According to incomplete data from the Chinese online newspaper *21st Century Business Herald*, since 2017 CATL has invested in 49 battery-related firms (see Appendix Table A1) in a wide variety of areas, essentially forming a business group, as do many successful Chinese firms.[49]

CATL has been the largest beneficiary of the transition to LFP batteries and is preparing for a potential transition to sodium-based batteries. CATL (2023) invested $2.3 billion in R&D in 2023, an increase of 18 percent over the level in 2022.[50] The transition away from nickel-based batteries has eroded the patent

---

[47] www.motortrend.com/features/public-ev-charging-stations-issues-problems-concerns/.
[48] https://restofworld.org/2024/vemo-byd-chinese-ev-charging-mexico/.
[49] https://baijiahao.baidu.com/s?id=1688954692503433215&wfr=spider&for=pc/.
[50] By comparison, SK Innovation, the largest Korean battery producer, invested $170 million in R&D.

Table 7 Location of global CATL factories, date established, and ownership

Facility	Location	Date established or planned opening	Ownership
Battery factory	Erfurt, Germany	2019	Wholly owned
Battery factory	Debrecen, Hungary	2025	Wholly owned
Cathode materials	Morocco	2024	Wholly owned
Battery factory	Spain	2024	JV Stellantis
Battery assembly	Thailand	2024	JV Arun Group
Mining, processing, battery manufacturing and recycling	Indonesia	2022	JV ANTAM and IBI
Battery factory	Michigan, US	2025	JV Ford (cancelled)
Factory equipment	Nevada, US	2025	Tesla factory

Source: Author compilation, 2024.

advantage of the Korean and Japanese producers. Moreover, CATL is rapidly building a global production footprint that will soon enable the firm to compete with the incumbent Korean and Japanese producers and circumvent potential trade-related restrictions. CATL is the global leader and appears to be increasing its advantage; its greatest competitor is BYD, which suggests that China is likely to become the future center of battery production.

4.3 Building Sources of Supply Other than China

As mentioned earlier, China is increasingly becoming the center of the EV value chain, creating a conundrum for traditional ICE automakers and their countries, if the transition to EVs continues on the current path. In that situation, China also becomes the center for the development and production of a variety of motor vehicles. The United States and Europe, which are trying to protect their incumbent ICE-related industries, will face many difficult decisions that might require subsidies and the possibility that those subsidies may have to be permanent, as the firms are increasingly confined to their protected domestic markets. For example,

US graphite producers requested the introduction of tariffs on Chinese imports (Rajagopal 2024) as a defensive protectionist strategy to enable the domestic industry to adjust.

4.4 Conclusion

China's investment in and development of a comprehensive domestically based value chain for EVs has evolved. Some Chinese firms, such as BYD, have built an entire vertically integrated EV supply chain, in some cases, establishing cross-holdings with firms within the supply chain ecosystem, as illustrated by our analysis of CATL's investment in a wide range of firms in its supply chain.

Equally important, in the early years of this process, the Chinese government invested in R&D not only in batteries but also in other key components. It also introduced local content regulations for EV assemblers, thereby further localizing production and building capabilities in China. Moreover, because this happened early in the development of the EV industry, China was not using legacy technologies but, rather, developing cutting-edge technologies.

The state of investment in and development of the EV supply chain is highly competitive in China and in many other countries, especially those with large ICE industries involving many jobs. It is too early to arrive at a final assessment of the direction of the global EV industry. But China is in the vanguard in terms of developing an EV supplier ecosystem that seemingly has no global rival. Because of both government encouragement and funding and their own competitive realities, all the actors in the Chinese EV supply chain are investing massively in R&D, which is directed at not only incremental innovation but also breakthroughs, such as the development of sodium-based batteries.

These suppliers will also benefit from the fact that batteries are an important general-purpose technology in a future based on electricity, one in which China seems likely to be at the center with respect to the supply of components.[51] Moreover, this supplier ecosystem (base) will make it very difficult for suppliers in smaller EV markets, such as the United States and the EU, to maintain their technological competitiveness. The emerging trade war might mean that successful non-Chinese suppliers of important EV components, such as Bosch and Magna, might become unintended victims of their own country's protectionism.

5 Globalization of the Chinese EV Industry

In a 2018 *Management and Organization Review* (MOR) article, David Teece (2018: 504) argued that "success in China ... is not necessarily a good predictor

---

[51] Also, Chinese catch-up and now leadership in alternative energy equipment, such as solar panels and wind turbines, allow even further integration of the entire alternative energy supply chain.

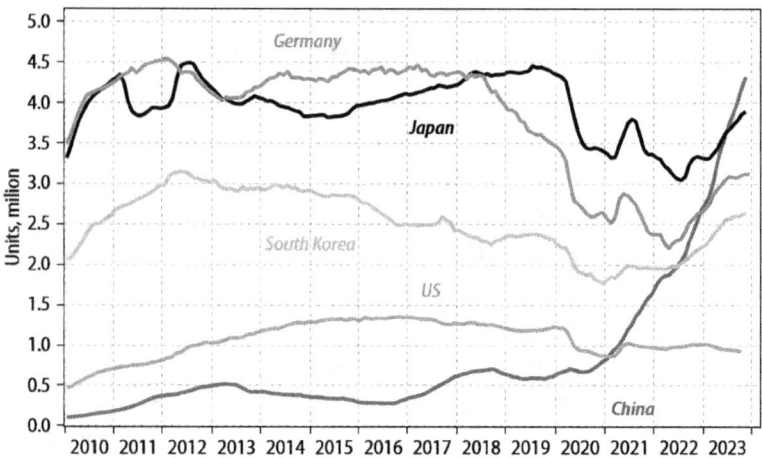

Figure 7 China has become an auto export powerhouse

Source: https://snippet.finance/china-car-exports/

of success globally." This observation was accurate before a massive shift among Chinese consumers to EVs, dramatic growth in EV manufacturing capacity, domestic market price competition, and continuing rapid improvements in battery technology. These developments were driving down the cost of Chinese-made EVs to the point at which they became less expensive to purchase and to operate than ICE vehicles. The rapid building of manufacturing capacity and accompanying fierce price competition that began in 2020 led both Chinese and Western automakers manufacturing EVs in China to look toward export markets (see Figure 7). At the time that this Element was written, Chinese manufacturers had no access to the US market, and the largest export destination for gasoline-powered vehicles from Japan, South Korea, and Germany remained the United States – a situation that Trump's newly enacted tariffs may affect.

An overlooked phenomenon is that Japanese used cars are popular in emerging markets in Asia, the Middle East, Africa, and Central and South America (excluding Mexico). This longtime market remains substantial, for example, the number of used Japanese cars exported to Africa in 2023 was 255,000, far exceeding the 92,000 new cars exported from China. And yet, as Figure 8 shows, Chinese exports continued to increase in 2024. The globalization of the Chinese EVs continues to be driven by exports. More recently, Chinese EV manufacturers followed Korean and Japanese ICE manufacturers by investing in assembly and manufacturing facilities in other countries.

As shown in Figure 9, China is exporting cars to a wide variety of countries. Some of these exports are produced in China by European manufacturers or by

The Demise of the Global ICE Industry 49

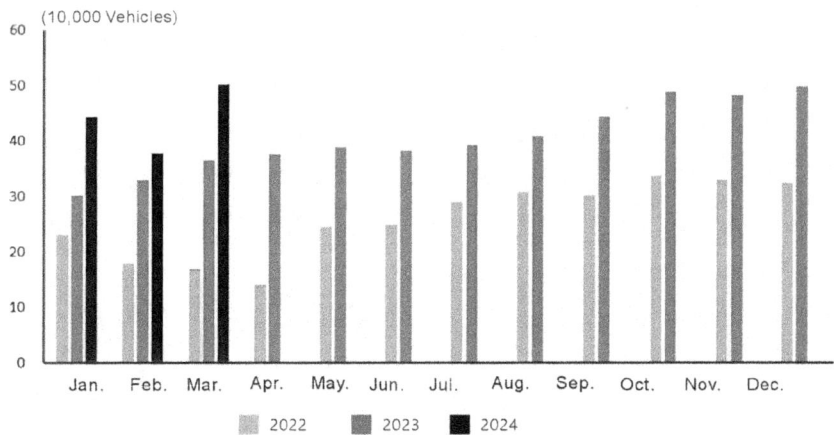

Figure 8 Monthly exports of automobiles from China, 2022–March 2024

Source: China Association of Automobile Manufacturers, as reported in Wondee Autoparts, Analysis of China's automobile exports in March 2024, April 22, 2024, www.wondee.com/Analysis-of-China-s-automobile-exports-in-March-2024-id48827486.html.

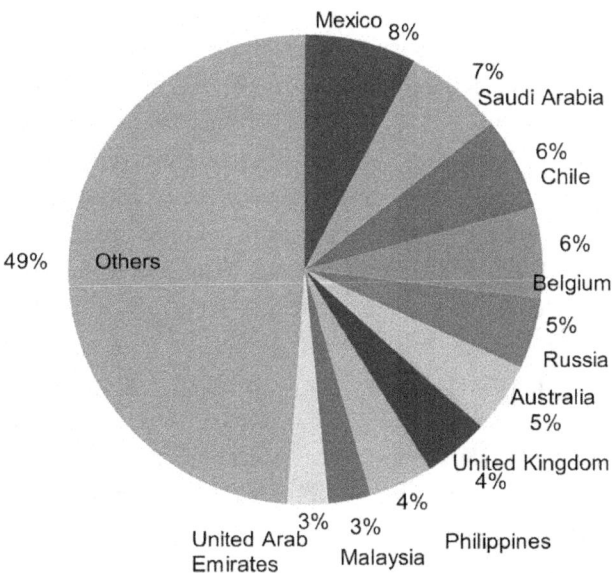

Figure 9 Top destinations of Chinese vehicle exports, 2022

Source: General Administration of Customs of China and China Association of Automobile Manufacturers, June 20, 2023.

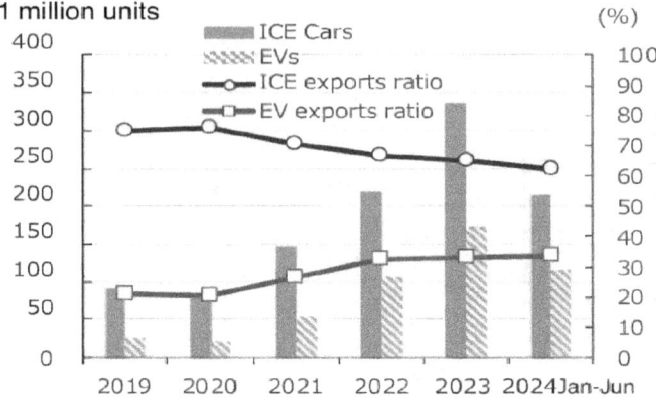

Figure 10 China's auto exports by category
Source: Miura (2024)

Tesla, destined for Europe and third countries. Norway is especially noteworthy, as in 2024, Chinese imports captured 15 percent of its market, according to Mallikka (2024). For example, Automotive News Europe (2024) reports that the BMW ix3, which is produced in China, is exported to Europe. Similarly, Tesla exports vehicles produced at its Shanghai Gigafactory to many countries. Further, Chinese exports to Oceania, especially Australia, are increasing rapidly (Kankai 2023). Also, helping Chinese exports are the Western sanctions on Russia.[52] In addition, in 2023 BYD entered the Japanese market, which has long been dominated by Japanese producers. Finally, Chinese firms are exporting commercial vehicles, especially buses to a number of countries. For example, electric buses produced by BYD operate in more than sixty countries and regions worldwide and have captured about 20 percent of the EV bus market in Europe, 70 percent in Japan, and more than 80 percent in the United States.

As Chinese firms push to achieve economies of scale, they are turning to exports as an outlet for this capacity. Responding to this export tsunami is difficult not only because of the low Chinese prices but also because of the size and speed of growth in this industry. The transition of the Chinese EV industry from an unimportant exporter to the largest exporter took only four years.[53]

On the other hand, Figure 10 shows that it is not EVs but internal combustion engine (ICE) vehicles that have made China the world's largest exporter of

---

[52] The role of Western sanctions on Russia should not be overlooked as an important contributor to Chinese automobile exports, as it opened one of the largest markets in the world that did not have an indigenous automotive industry. For example, in 2023 Chinese automobile exports to Russia totaled $11.6 billion and comprised 15 percent of the Chinese auto exports, according to Vorotnikov (2024).

[53] To transport all these automobiles, Chinese auto manufacturers have ordered record numbers of automobile carrier ships (Asia Financial 2024).

automobiles. According to the China Automobile Dealers Association, ICE vehicles accounted for 64.9 percent of China's total vehicle exports (passenger cars plus buses, trucks, and vans) in 2023, significantly higher than the 33.3 percent share of EVs. This unique fact confirms our view in Section 3 that the success of China's electric vehicles was not driven by the global export market, but was first and foremost aimed at the domestic market and had received strong support from the government. This is also in contrast to other Asian counterparts such as Japan and South Korea. In these countries, one of the main triggers behind the success of their auto industry as a global player was the large-scale export of automobiles, particularly to the North American market.

Chinese EV and battery firms are not only expanding exports but building or exploring production facilities in other countries. The clear leader in offshoring production is BYD, which opened a bus factory in Lancaster, California, in 2017 and in Newmarket, Canada. Three factories are making various products in Brazil and, in 2019, two in Europe (Hungary and France). BYD has also expressed interest in an auto factory in Mexico as an entry into the North American market – but in 2025 this was put on hold due to the uncertainty created by the Trump administration. In 2010, the Zhejiang Geely Holding Group acquired the Swedish-based Volvo brand as well as Lotus and operates factories in Sweden, and SAIC owns the MG brand (formerly a British brand). These developments suggest that Chinese EV manufacturers are rapidly gaining experience in operating in overseas markets.

The rapid growth of EV production in China and exports has also led Chinese firms to open production facilities in other countries. This is surprising because, as late as 2018, Teece and others argued that overseas operations require dynamic capabilities, rather than ordinary capabilities, to overcome the "liability of newness" (Stinchcombe 1965) and speculated that Chinese firms might find it challenging to do so. They believed that Chinese automakers, most of which at that time were focused on their domestic ICE market and had relatively weak global brands, would require many years to establish recognition of their brands in other countries. However, the intense domestic competition and cost advantages incentivized Chinese EV manufacturers to expand into the global market. In response, both the United States and the European Union have adopted defensive strategies intended to give domestic manufacturers time to catch up. These strategies consist of punitive tariffs and the exclusion of imports of Chinese-made cars – to the point that even exports to their home countries by German automakers and Tesla are likely to be banned.

At the same time, Chinese EV producers are working rapidly to export to and even manufacture in developing countries in Southeast Asia, Latin America, and Africa that lack a domestic auto industry and have large and growing markets (Tanabe 2024). The number of new gas-powered cars exported from China in 2020 was a mere 570,000, compared to 2.414 million exported from Japan.

However, the EV disruption has changed the landscape and made it possible for Chinese EV firms to bring EVs to market with prices at or below those of ICE vehicles. As the transition to EVs continues, the potential for China to become the global leader in manufacturing motor vehicles is a development that established ICE producers and their home countries must address, given the economic and political consequences, such as the growing impact on high-wage auto workers. However, it may be too early to predict the takeover of overseas automotive producers by Chinese-made EVs. Most of the cars exported overseas are manufactured in China. Due to overcapacity and domestic competition, Chinese auto manufacturers are being forced to expand their overseas manufacturing bases, but most of these initiatives are still in the planning or knock-down (CKD) manufacturing stages. In this sense, the prediction by Teece (2018) may still be accurate.

6 Conclusion: The Transformation of the Global Automotive Industry

The precipitous growth of the EV industry in China and its rise to global leadership have been nothing short of astounding and could not have been predicted a decade ago. In this Element, we show that this growth was propelled by a series of Chinese central government initiatives embedded in several five-year plans that directed attention and initially modest resources to a vaguely defined idea of "new energy" vehicles. These initiatives interacted synergistically with the emergence of a large number of new entrepreneurs and intense interprovincial competition, which drove local governments' NEV support. This complex combination of initiatives by the central and local governments and the surge of entrepreneurial initiative enabled China to become a leader in both production and increasingly innovation in this rapidly developing industry. It also is leading to the obsolescence of industries that have relied on the ICE, even as batteries have become one of the most important general-purpose technologies of the early twenty-first century.

Although China's EVs were initially introduced by BYD at around the same time as the appearance of the first Tesla model, Tesla attracted far more attention in both China and the United States. Before 2018, Tesla was publicly well known, even though few Teslas were on the road, but around 2018, commercialization of EVs began to accelerate. It is now evident that China has emerged as the epicenter of the global EV industry and its supply chain. More important,

China is becoming a major driver of R&D advances in every aspect of EVs, as acknowledged in a report by the European Union (EU) (Bielewski et al. 2023). Beginning in 2023, the reaction in the EU, the United States, and Japan to Chinese success became one of panic.

Given the massive scale of corporate investment and central government incentives in China as well as its dynamic scientific and engineering innovation ecosystem, Chinese firms, led by CATL and BYD and joined by Xpeng and other less-well-known suppliers, are charging ahead and, in the process, defining various aspects of EV technologies. Hence, China is increasingly leading the transition to what might be called the "battery era." Initially, the established ICE manufacturers in Europe, Korea, Japan, and the United States had announced aggressive strategies for producing EVs, but in 2024 they changed course, adopting defensive measures to slow the penetration of their markets of Chinese EVs. In Germany, the unanticipated and rapid global adoption of EVs drove down sales by Volkswagen, which announced its urgent need to lay off workers and close factories.[54] Honda, Nissan, and Toyota are shuttering ICE factories in China and elsewhere. Ford has gone through several strategies in its attempts to counter Chinese competitors. According to a confidential interview with a longtime president of one of the largest Ford dealers in the US Southern states, the company asked leading dealers to carry Ford EVs and required them to invest $1 million to be able to sell and service these EVs. Soon, Ford reversed its optimistic sales forecast and reverted its product mix to ICE vehicles, representing the abandonment of its EV strategy just as Chinese EV producers were ramping up their plans for global market expansion.

As Ford began to retreat, General Motors and Stellantis pivoted their emphasis to plug-in hybrids (PHEVs), which became attractive because of range anxiety. The lack of charging infrastructure in the United States made range a major disincentive for many prospective purchasers of EVs, a problem that was mitigated by PHEVs. Chinese manufacturers had also recognized the upside of PHEVs and offered a broad variety of them in the domestic and foreign markets. As a stop-gap measure, Toyota introduced an engine of much lower weight than that of a standard ICE vehicle and that can continuously charge the car battery, thereby accommodating larger battery packs with the engine as a backup if the batteries fully discharged.[55] Having an EV that can be powered by both batteries and internal combustion is inherently costlier than having one powered only by batteries – hence, it is likely to be a transitional technology in the evolution to vehicles that overcome the driving range of EVs.

---

[54] www.reuters.com/business/autos-transportation/volkswagen-goes-head-to-head-with-work force-over-proposed-company-cuts-2024-09-04/.
[55] www.ecoticias.com/en/toyota-hydrogen-engines-new-models/4195/.

These developments are occurring in the context of increasingly severe shocks from climate change and the global goal to achieve "net zero" scenarios, which is increasing the belief that zero-emission vehicles will be necessary. It is the goal of many countries in the EU as well as states such as California that by 2038 sales of ICE cars will end in many leading markets. According to Bloomberg (2024), almost every country will actively adopt or consider decarbonization solutions by the early 2030s. EVs are vital for the success of this effort. As a result of global economic and political changes, increasingly significant markets for EVs are being created not only in developed countries but in Latin America, Africa, and Asia and in countries such as India, Mexico, Russia, and South Africa. Many Chinese companies (e.g., BYD, Geely, Chery, SAIC, and Chang'an) offer low-cost EVs and have become large-scale exporters to Brazil, Chile, and Mexico as well as countries in Eastern Europe. The impact on Germany, Japan, and South Korea, the major auto exporters, is already considerable and will increase.

In addition, Chinese manufacturers are actively exploring the opening of manufacturing operations in the EU (e.g., in Spain and Eastern Europe) and Mexico (for the Mexican market and exports to the United States and Canada). Moreover, Tesla and some European ICE automakers with production facilities in China are leveraging China's cost advantages to export not only to their home markets but also to third countries in Southeast Asia and the Middle East.

China and its EV manufacturers are rapidly changing the geopolitical configuration of global auto production. To illustrate, BYD was transformed from a battery company into a vertically integrated EV manufacturer. In many respects, BYD's growing global presence symbolizes the auto industry's shift to EVs and the emergence of many new Chinese brand names as well as new supply chains of Chinese EV component providers. In June 2024, BYD's sales jumped 35 percent in China as it initiated price competition by introducing successive price reduction strategies across its entire product line; as a result, Honda and other foreign competitors that could not match these reductions experienced double-digit slumps in sales.

The challenge is not confined to China. For example, Honda plans to cut its manufacturing capacity by 50 percent in Thailand, where BYD is emerging as a market leader. BYD is also planning to open several overseas plants as it expands its global manufacturing footprint and seeks to circumvent prohibitive tariffs. For example, in 2024 it opened its first plant in Thailand, and plants are in place or under construction in Hungary, Spain, Brazil, Turkey, Mexico, and Pakistan.[56] Michael Dunne, a veteran of the automotive industry, stated

---

[56] https://electrek.co/2024/08/16/byd-plots-another-ev-plant-why-a-big-deal/.

apocalyptically that, in 2024, China had initiated a global car blitzkrieg.[57] China was expected to export as many as six million passenger vehicles (made by both Chinese and Western firms) to more than a hundred countries in 2024, cementing its position as the world's number one auto exporter and the global leader in EVs.

If the current trajectory continues, the rapid growth and increasing global centrality of the Chinese EV and battery industries will change the configuration of global automotive production. The transition to EVs has enabled Chinese firms to launch a wide range of cars, including luxury vehicles, supercars, and entry-level models, effectively upending the established ICE manufacturers, which are in the unfamiliar position of having to catch up with China in EVs. None of the established ICE automakers have formulated or expressed a strategy for gaining an advantage over China. Moreover, the emergence of the Chinese EV industry is most remarkable for the speed with which it has attained global prominence.

In 2018, few would have predicted such success by 2024, at a time when European and US automakers saw Tesla as a curiosity, not as a future competitor, and considered the transition to a dominant EV industry many years in the future. However, in 2024 it became glaringly obvious that China was unconcerned about complaints by the industries and governments elsewhere concerning what they believed was Chinese excess capacity and size as the world's largest auto exporter. Therefore, concerns in the United States, the EU, South Korea, and Japan shifted dramatically to a fear that the transition to a renewable future would be dominated by Chinese industry and that the manufacturing of automobiles, an important pillar of the G-7 economies, would be overtaken by China.

6.1 Top-down Government Action and Bottom-up Entrepreneurial Action

The growth and dynamism in the Chinese EV industry is the result of a unique interaction among government policy initiatives, competition between some entrepreneurial provinces and cities such as Shenzhen and Hefei, and many startup companies that have introduced a host of EV technologies and car designs. Many leading Chinese EV and battery firms – such as NIO, BYD, and CATL – benefited from subsidies extended by the central and local governments and policy initiatives, such as preferential licensing of EVs in large cities and purchases of municipal government fleets of buses and taxis. Although these benefits are not unique (e.g., Tesla took advantage of myriad government programs in the United States), a large number of entrepreneurs went into the

---

[57] https://newsletter.dunneinsights.com/p/the-great-china-car-blitzkrieg/.

EV industry because of these subsidies. And yet in China only a few of the many entrants survived the fierce competition to become world-class competitors.

Moreover, beginning with the twelfth FYP (2011–2015), Chinese government policy comprised a series of "new energy initiatives," which evolved as the industry grew. First, government policy deliberately aimed to create an industrial ecosystem, such as by encouraging the building of a global supply chain for critical raw materials (e.g., lithium deposits outside China) as well as end-of-life recycling. This policy was dynamic, as the incentives for all actors from the customer to lithium miners were continuously tweaked to achieve various goals. China managed to become a leader not only in LFP battery technology but also in sodium battery technology.

Second, government policy evolved. For example, after some serious malfeasance in the distribution of subsidies, the government mandated testing of EVs to certify which auto models and batteries qualified for subsidies. Then it gradually increased the performance specifications for qualification, thereby pressuring the industry to improve performance. In evolutionary terms, it created a selection environment that delivered greater battery performance, including higher battery power density, better packaging, solid-state battery designs that eliminated liquid processes, and increasingly rapid charging.

Third, policy reflected a strategic decision to push joint venture ICE companies in China to enter the China EV market as a way to stimulate growth in a component and technology supply chain. Most important was the decision to allow Tesla to build a wholly owned Gigafactory in Shanghai. The clear goal was to force Chinese firms to compete and learn from the firm that was the global leader and would become their competitor.

6.2 Implications for the World

ICE automakers are facing increasing pressure to switch to EVs because of more stringent environmental regulations worldwide and political and government commitments. These commitments include the formation of the Zero Emission Alliance by nineteen countries and dozens of automakers at the COP26 conference in Glasgow in 2021, with the common goal of completing the transition by 2035–2040. The legacy ICE manufacturers are planning to transition their operations to a world in which EVs are the dominant type of automobile, but this transition is proving to be challenging. All the major players – including General Motors, Toyota, Ford, Mercedes-Benz, BMW, Stellantis, and Hyundai – have scaled back their ambition to transition to EVs, despite the widespread belief that EVs will ultimately dominate the market. However, some, such as Toyota, are still unconvinced that battery-powered automobiles will be the ultimate solution.

But pivoting from their profitable ICE business and, at the same time, implementing a catch-up strategy has been difficult, leading every ICE automaker to announce a sharp retreat from its timetable of only three years ago. For example, Volkswagen's strong lobbying for EVs in the EU opened rifts between the company and some other EU automakers, which considered the transition a fundamental threat that would devalue many of their legacy capabilities. In many respects, Volkswagen faced a conflict, as it had to adopt an aggressive electrification strategy after having bet on "clean" diesel engines – a strategy that had lost all credibility after the company was found to have cheated on emissions tests. In response, Volkswagen announced an ambitious volte-face to develop EVs. Manufacturers in many countries made overly optimistic sales projections (which some observers described as wishful thinking) that failed to be met. However, this was not the case in China, where 51.1 percent of the cars sold in July 2024 were EVs (BEVs and PHEVS), exceeded the following month, as EV sales outpaced those of ICE vehicles, and the share rose to 53 percent.

It appears that, in the United States and in most of the EU, Tesla's success was due to the appeal to early adopters, who were willing to learn and adapt to the comparatively short range of early nickel-cobalt batteries, the inadequate charging infrastructure in the United States and, to a lesser extent, the EU. R&D and innovation in EVs and batteries are currently in a period of great ferment and technological development. In 2024, James Farley, the CEO of Ford, took a tour of EV manufacturers in China and afterward gave voice to a rapidly emerging consensus that what automakers had to do in the future was to design and produce PHEVs that would combine an ICE and batteries.

Most recent forecasts of the future US EV market assume that buyers will prefer PHEVs until the time comes that batteries can achieve an acceptable range (e.g., over 300 miles). Technology that eliminates drivers' range anxiety about traveling long distances has great potential. For example, Volkswagen demonstrated that its ID7 Pro S model can travel almost 500 miles on a single charge, further raising expectations about driving range.[58] Technological competition over designing better batteries is expected to intensify to improve energy density and thus range, charging speed, and lowering cost. For example, in June 2024, CATL, the Chinese battery giant, announced a battery that could be recharged over 4,000 times and could operate for 1.2 million miles – exceeding the life of any ICE vehicle by far.[59] And, everyday, there new

---

[58] www.gbnews.com/lifestyle/cars/volkswagen-destroys-range-anxiety-fears-electric-car-battery-range/.

[59] https://insideevs.com/news/726654/catl-long-servicelife-battery-16years-2million-kilometers/#:~:text=According%20to%20CATL%2C%20its%20%22Long,That's%20a%20lot%20of%20driving .

announcements of technological improvements in battery energy density, range, life expectancy, charging times, and, above all, cost.

In the near term, Western governments are likely to adopt defensive industrial policies, such as tariffs and local content regulations, which are intended to impede or slow Chinese imports. The US strategy of tariffs appears to be based on the hope that it will enable the creation of strong new competitors for battery services, such as replacing/switching batteries on demand (which resembles the successful model that NIO introduced in China). Of course, the Chinese government is determined to contest and counteract these tariffs. In 2024, the EU undertook an extensive investigation of China's subsidies and documented the extent to which direct subsidies and various incentives helped Chinese EV manufacturers to become global low-cost leaders; the subsidies supported massive automation in car assembly using techniques, such as giga-casting, which was pioneered by Tesla. BMW has also turned to automation, testing an approach (including the use of humanoid robots) in production lines that might apply to future EV models.[60]

The strategy by the EU and the United States consists of imposing very high tariffs on Chinese EVs in order to protect their domestic manufacturers, but it is too soon to say whether this approach will be effective. Nor is it clear that their strategy includes consideration of China's potential response, which might be an attempt to dominate not just the low end but the luxury models that would present the most competition to EU and US brands, including Tesla.

IG Metall, the German metalworkers' union (and unions in other European countries), is extremely concerned that the transition to EVs will result in significant redundancies – a concern that is reinforced by Volkswagen's closure of some factories in Germany, as mentioned earlier. Similar concerns are shared by labor as well as firm executives in the United States, who worry that the entry of low-cost Chinese EVs will decimate the market share of their products. In some respects, the introduction of Chinese EV manufacturers to the global market resembles that of Japanese automakers, which entered the global market on the basis of a superior production system. The success of Chinese automakers might be even more disruptive, as it is predicated on batteries with a new dominant design, based on lithium iron phosphate batteries (LFP).

6.3 The Race for Future Batteries

Batteries are at the heart of the electric vehicles expected to dominate in the future. Their performance and safety can be improved at all links of the supply chain: electrode and electrolyte materials, electrodes and other cell components,

---

[60] www.greencarcongress.com/2022/05/20220501-ifactory.html.

battery cells, modules, packs, and battery management systems. China leads the United States and Europe in the production of batteries, in which it has a competitive advantage due to its homegrown supply chain. Not only is the manufacturing of battery cells concentrated in China but so is the production of key battery components, such as cathodes, anodes, separators, and electrolytes.

Over the past decade, Chinese companies have rapidly emerged as global players, challenging established battery manufacturers (Samsung, LG, Panasonic, etc.) and materials suppliers (Umicore, Sumitomo Metal Mining, etc.). Although in 2020 nickel-based batteries made up more than 90 percent of the EV battery market, at present, improvements in LFP technology have enabled it to dominate the EV market. Chinese battery manufacturers, in particular, lead in the development of LFP battery chemistry and displacement of nickel-based batteries. The continuous advancement of electrification technology has led to the emergence of a new generation of battery technologies. For example, researchers at the Massachusetts Institute of Technology claim to have developed a new technology that can increase the energy density of lithium-ion batteries by 60 percent. On the other hand, to alleviate charging anxiety, recently, in March 2025, BYD unveiled a new five-minute battery charging system that can travel 400 kilometers (249 miles) on a five-minute charge, which is twice as fast as a Tesla's Superchargers.

In recent years, the competitive and technological landscape of solid-state batteries has shifted, as numerous startups as well as ICE legacy manufacturers have joined the fray (Toyota, Nissan, Hyundai/Kia, Honda, General Motors, etc.). In particular, companies from the United States, Europe, Japan, and South Korea – which lagged behind China in LFP batteries – are pinning their hopes on next-generation battery technology. Toyota and Samsung are both reported to be planning a commercial release of their solid-state batteries in 2027. CATL also announced its intention to produce solid-state batteries in small lots in 2027. This suggests that the competition to develop improved rechargeable batteries will continue.

It is also reasonable to expect continuing innovation in the design and production of EVs, as engineers continue to optimize vehicles based on batteries. This has already led to the structural redesign of cars and their production. For example, innovations such as incorporating batteries into the car body could significantly decrease the weight, increase safety, and simplify manufacture.[61] Tesla pioneered this redesign in manufacturing by introducing the giga-press. Further innovations in this realm should be expected, as designers and engineers

---

[61] www.macheforum.com/site/threads/carmakers-want-to-ditch-battery-packs-use-auto-bodies-for-energy-storage.1958/.

come to understand what is possible. China and Chinese firms seem increasingly likely to capture the economic benefits of these innovations.

In addition, active developments in robotics and automated assembly of EVs will reduce labor costs and expand the use of automated assembly. Drivetrain efficiency is likely to rise as electrical motors improve, and advancements are achieved in other dimensions, such as the proper positioning of these motors for maximum efficiency. Components such as tires, suspension, and brakes that are common to ICE vehicles and EVs will continue to evolve, as they are optimized for EVs. If China remains the center of the global EV industry and continues to have the most dynamic EV innovation ecosystem, Chinese firms in all these sectors are likely to become dominant, particularly because of massive R&D investment by them and the government.

If we are entering an "electric future," then batteries will be the main general-purpose technology – one in which, at present, the United States and Europe not only have less manufacturing capacity but also increasingly lag behind China, especially in terms of R&D capacity. Moreover, the knowledge accumulating because of EV success can be repurposed not only for energy storage but for all other activities that require energy. In the process, the knowledge collected by firms about ICE for over a century will become obsolete. For example, CATL announced that it has developed a battery-powered airplane.[62] This demonstrates that the EV revolution increasingly resembles the transformation of society wrought by the ICE – a transformation that began in the 1860s and drove a global shift that ultimately enabled the rise of the United States after the 1930s, as what many called "Fordism" became a way of organizing society based on mass production and mass consumption. This dynamic enabled the automobile industry and petrochemicals to become the principal industries in the most powerful member countries of the Organisation for Economic Co-operation and Development (the United States, Japan, Germany, France, Italy, and, later, South Korea). In this respect, if EVs become dominant, China's apparent success in EVs and the technologies it enables could, in part, be an important factor in escaping the middle-income trap and augurs a fundamental global geopolitical realignment. In this case, for countries, such as Germany and Japan, in which ICE production has been central to their fortunes, very difficult times lie ahead.

---

[62] https://newatlas.com/aircraft/catl-worlds-largest-ev-battery-manufacturer-aircraft/.

References

Abernathy, W. J. (1978). *The Productivity Dilemma*. Johns Hopkins University Press.

Asia Financial (2024). China firms order dozens of ships for EV, exports surge. (April 10). www.asiafinancial.com/china-firms-order-dozens-of-ships-for-ev-exports-surge/.

Automotive News Europe (2024). Mercedes, BMW, VW criticize EU's high tariffs on Chinese EV imports. (June 12). https://europe.autonews.com/automakers/german-automakers-slam-eus-high-tariffs-chinese-ev-exports/.

AutoVista (2025a). China starts 2025 at the front of the global EV market. (March 28). https://autovista24.autovistagroup.com/news/china-starts-2025-at-the-front-of-the-global-ev-market/.

AutoVista (2025b). Which brand sold the most EVs in Europe in 2024? (February 20). https://autovista24.autovistagroup.com/news/which-brand-sold-the-most-evs-in-europe-in-2024/.

Bielewski, M., Pfrang, A., Quintero Pulido, D. et al. (2023). Clean energy technology observatory: Battery technology in the European Union. 2023 status report on technology development, trends, value chains and markets. Publications Office of the European Union. https://doi.org/10.2760/52259, JRC135406.

Bloomberg (2024). Nio loses another $2.9 billion as China's EV battle heats up. (March 5). www.bloomberg.com/news/articles/2024-03-05/nio-full-year-losses-widen-as-pressure-mounts-in-china-ev-market/.

Bosch (2024). Our worldwide research and advance engineering locations. (April 16). www.bosch.com/research/about-bosch-research/research-locations/.

Cao, Y. (2024). China's charging pile expertise sought-after in overseas countries. *China Daily* (April 22). www.chinadaily.com.cn/a/202404/22/WS6625c372a31082fc043c3329.html.

CATL (2023). Pursuing sustainable growth through a value-centered approach: Dr. Robin Zeng. (June 27). www.catl.com/en/news/6256.html#:~:text=In%202023%2C%20CATL%20invested%20about,billion%20U.S.%20dollars)%20in%20R%26D/.

Christensen, C. M. (2013). *The Innovator's Dilemma: When New Technologies Cause Great Firms to Fail*. Harvard Business Review Press.

Chu, W. W. (2011). How the Chinese government promoted a global automobile industry. *Industrial and Corporate Change*, 20(5), 1235–1276.

Cox Automotive (2025). Electric vehicle sales jump higher in Q4, pushing U.S. sales to a record 1.3 million. (January 13). www.coxautoinc.com/market-insights/q4-2024-ev-sales/.

Deloitte (2021). Rethinking auto semiconductor strategy in an uncertain era. (November). https://www2.deloitte.com/cn/en/pages/consumer-business/articles/automotive-semiconductors-strategic.html.

Goldman Sachs. (2024). Electric vehicle battery prices are expected to fall almost 50% by 2026. (October 7). www.goldmansachs.com/insights/articles/electric-vehicle-battery-prices-are-expected-to-fall-almost-50-percent-by-2025.

Economy, E. (2014). China's round two on electric cars: Will it work? *Forbes* (April 18). www.forbes.com/sites/elizabetheconomy/2014/04/18/chinas-round-two-onelectric-cars-will-it-work/#2b66c52f5573/.

Gong, H., & Hansen, T. (2023). The rise of China's new energy vehicle lithium-ion battery industry: The coevolution of battery technological innovation systems and policies. *Environmental Innovation and Societal Transitions*, 46, 100689.

Gong, H., Wang, M. Q., & Wang, H. (2013). New energy vehicles in China: Policies, demonstration, and progress. *Mitigation and Adaptation Strategies for Global Change*, 18, 207–228.

Graham, J. D., Belton, K. B., & Xia, S. (2021). How China beat the US in electric vehicle manufacturing. *Issues in Science and Technology*, 37(2), 72–79.

Han, X., Liu, W., & Jiang, T. (2024). Practising *future*-making: Anticipation and translocal politics of Tesla's Gigafactory in Shanghai as assemblage. *Transactions of the Institute of British Geographers*, 49, e12645. Available from: https://doi.org/10.1111/tran.12645.

Hankook (2024). EV tires: Standing at inflection point. www.hankooktire.com/global/en/tech-in-motion/ev-tire.html.

Helveston, J. P., Wang, Y., Karplus, V. J., & Fuchs, E. R. (2019). Institutional complementarities: The origins of experimentation in China's plug-in electric vehicle industry. *Research Policy*, 48(1), 206–222.

Hirsch, J. (2015). Elon Musk's growing empire is fueled by $4.9 billion in government subsidies. *Los Angeles Times* (May 30). www.latimes.com/business/la-fi-hy-musk-subsidies-20150531-story.html.

Howell, S. T. (2018). Joint ventures and technology adoption: A Chinese industrial policy that backfired. *Research Policy*, 47(8), 1448–1462.

International Energy Agency (2022a). Global EV Outlook 2022: Securing supplies for an electric future. www.iea.org/reports/global-ev-outlook2022%0A https://iea.blob.core.windows.net/assets/ad8fb04c-4f75-42fc-973a6e54c8a4449a/GlobalElectricVehicleOutlook2022.pdf.

International Energy Agency (2022b). Global supply chains of EV batteries. (July). www.iea.org/reports/global-supply-chains-of-ev-batteries/.

International Energy Agency (2023). Trends in charging infrastructure. www.iea.org/reports/global-ev-outlook-2023/trends-in-charging-infrastructureis/.

Jiang, H., & Lu, F. (2023). New industry paradigms may overwhelm dynamic capabilities: Different competitive dynamics around Tesla and Chinese EV start-ups. *Management and Organization Review*, 19(1), 157–169.

Jin, L. Z., He, H., Cui H.Y. et al. (2021). Driving a green future: A retrospective review of China's electric vehicle development and outlook for the future. International Council on Clean Transportation. (January 14). https://theicct.org/publication/driving-a-green-future-a-retrospective-review-of-chinas-electric-vehicle-development-and-outlook-for-the-future/.

Kanger, L., Geels, F. W., Sovacool, B., & Schot, J. (2019). Technological diffusion as a process of societal embedding: Lessons from historical automobile transitions for future electric mobility. *Transportation Research Part D: Transport and Environment*, 71, 47–66.

Kankai, M. (2023). Chinese EVs gain in Japanese automakers' key markets. *Nikkei* (July 8). https://asia.nikkei.com/Business/Automobiles/Chinese-EVs-gain-in-Japanese-automakers-key-markets/.

Kenney, M., & Florida, R. (1993). *Beyond Mass Production: The Japanese System and Its Transfer to the US*. Oxford University Press.

Lienert, P. (2022). Exclusive: Automakers to double spending on EVs, batteries to $1.2 trillion by 2030. www.reuters.com/technology/exclusive-automakers-double-spending-evs-batteries-12-trillion-by-2030-2022-10-21/.

Lewin, A. Y., Kenney, M., & Murmann, J. P. (2016). *China's Innovation Challenge: Overcoming the Middle-Income Trap*. Cambridge University Press.

Liu, T. (2007). Wang Chuanfu: The power of a techno-maniac. *Chinese Entrepreneurs* 22. www.sina.com.cn.

Liu, Y. Q. (2024). *Research on Innovation and Development of China's New Energy Vehicle Industry*. Science Press (in Chinese).

Lu, C., Rong, K., You, J., & Shi, Y. (2014). Business ecosystem and stakeholders' role transformation: Evidence from Chinese emerging electric vehicle industry. *Expert Systems with Applications*, 41(10), 4579–4595.

MacDuffie, J. P. (2018). Response to Perkins and Murmann: Pay attention to what is and isn't unique about Tesla. *Management and Organization Review*, 14(3), 481–489.

Mallikka, M. (2024). The Norwegian market embraces Chinese EV brand. (January 12). https://scandasia.com/the-norwegian-market-embraces-chinese-ev-brands/.

Magna (2017). News Release: Magna forms e-powertrain joint venture in China. www.magna.com/company/newsroom/releases-archive/release/2017/10/18/news-release–magna-forms-e-powertrain-joint-venture-in-china/.

McKinsey (2021). Why the automotive future is electric. (September). www.mckinsey.com/~/media/mckinsey/industries/automotive%20and%20assembly/our%20insights/why%20the%20automotive%20future%20is%20electric/why-the-automotive-future-is-electric-f.pdf?shouldIndex=false/.

McKinsey (2023). Automotive powertrain suppliers face a rapidly electrifying future. (March). www.mckinsey.com/industries/automotive-and-assembly/our-insights/automotive-powertrain-suppliers-face-a-rapidly-electrifying-future.

Ministry of Industry and Information Technology (2017). China's new energy vehicle sales will account for more than 20% of total sales in 2025. www.gov.cn/xinwen/2017-01/15/content_5160009.htm.

Miura, Yushi. (2024). The global market from the perspective of China's auto industry, Research Focus (in Japanese). The Japan Research Institute. www.jri.co.jp.

Moore, G. A. (2014). *Crossing the Chasm: Marketing and Selling High-Tech Goods to Mainstream Customers*. Harper Business.

Mom, G. (2013). *The Electric Vehicle: Technology and Expectations in the Automobile Age*. JHU Press.

Mui, S. (2023). U.S. races ahead in EV manufacturing investments. NRDC (January 27). www.nrdc.org/bio/simon-mui/us-races-ahead-ev-manufacturing-investments/.

Murmann, J. P., & Vogt, F. (2023). A capabilities framework for dynamic competition: Assessing the relative chances of incumbents, start-ups, and diversifying entrants. *Management and Organization Review*, 19(1), 141–156.

O'Donovan, A. (2024). Electrified transport market outlook 4Q 2023: Growth ahead. (January 4). https://about.bnef.com/blog/electrified-transport-market-outlook-4q-2023-growth-ahead/.

Perkins, G., & Murmann, J. P. (2018). What does the success of Tesla mean for the future dynamics in the global automobile sector? *Management and Organization Review*, 14(3), 471–480.

Qiong, Y. (2017). Seven Chinese automakers punished for electric-vehicle subsidy fraud. (February 2). https://news.cgtn.com/news/3d51544e77496a4d/share_p.html.

Rajagopal, D. (2024). Graphite miners lobby US govt to impose levy on China-sourced EV material. Reuters (April 30). www.reuters.com/markets/commod

ities/graphite-miners-lobby-us-govt-impose-levy-china-sourced-ev-material-2024-04-30/.

Ren, D. (2018). Shenzhen's all-electric bus fleet is a world's first that comes with massive government funding. *South China Morning Post* (October 23). www.scmp.com/business/china-business/article/2169709/shenzhens-all-electric-bus-fleet-worlds-first-comes-massive/.

Shu, E. (2022). Paradoxical framing and coping process on sustainable new product development. *Technovation*, 111: 102392. https://doi.org/10.1016/j.technovation.2021.102392.

Sohu (2017). We've already had two practices of going from 0 to achieving the largest scale. (November 15). www.sohu.com/a/204449371_114778/.

State Council (2012). Energy saving and new energy automobile industry, 2012-2020. (June 28). www.gov.cn/gongbao/content/2012/content_2182749.htm.

Stinchcombe, A. L. (1965). Social structure and organizations. In March, J. P. (Ed.), *Handbook of Organizations*. Rand McNally, 142–193.

Stringham, E. P., Miller, J. K., & Clark, J. R. (2015). Overcoming barriers to entry in an established industry: Tesla Motors. *California Management Review*, 57(4), 85–103.

Sun, J., & Kenney, M. (2024). Mobilizing local governments to build global class innovative industries: Reconsidering the Chinese National Innovation System. https://ssrn.com/abstract=4766927; http://dx.doi.org/10.2139/ssrn.4766927.

Tanabe, S. (2024). China EV makers Neta, Xpeng turn to Africa amid European backlash. *Nikkei Asia* (July 3). https://asia.nikkei.com/Spotlight/Electric-cars-in-China/China-EV-makers-Neta-Xpeng-turn-to-Africa-amid-European-backlash/.

Teece, D. J. (2018). Tesla and the reshaping of the auto industry. *Management and Organization Review*, 14(3), 501–512. https://doi.org/10.1017/mor.2018.33.

Teece, D. J., Pisano, G., & Shuen, A. (1997). Dynamic capabilities and strategic management. *Strategic Management Journal*, 18(7), 509–533.

Utterback, J. M., & Suárez, F. F. (1993). Innovation, competition, and industry structure. *Research Policy*, 22(1), 1–21.

Vorotnikov, V. (2024). Chinese finished vehicle exports to Russia in jeopardy (June 20). www.automotivelogistics.media/trade-and-customs/chinese-finished-vehicle-exports-to-russia-in-jeopardy/45782.article#:~:text=In%202023%2C%20Chinese%20finished%20vehicle,market%20%E2%80%93%20the%20highest%20figure%20ever/.

Wang, J. Y., Liu, Y. Q., & Kokko, A. (2012). Comparative study on the policies and effects of the "Ten Cities, One Thousand Vehicles" demonstration project. *Scientific Decision Making*, no. 12, 1–14. (in Chinese).

Wang, S. (2022). Leap Motor, eager to lead. JieMian News.com (September 23). www.jiemian.com/article/8118610.html.

Weinert, J., Ma, C., & Cherry, C. (2007). The transition to electric bikes in China: history and key reasons for rapid growth. *Transportation*, 34, 301–318.

Wilmot, S. (2023). Toyota's hybridized EV strategy is expensive. *Wall Street Journal* (May 10). www.wsj.com/articles/toyotas-hybridized-ev-strategy-is-expensive-e9a62667/.

Yan, F., & Dou, M. (2016). What does an incomplete list of companies engaged in new energy vehicle subsidy fraud mean? *People's Daily Online* (September 11). http://auto.people.com.cn/n1/2016/0911/c1005-28706880.html.

Yeung, G. (2019). "Made in China 2025": The development of a new energy vehicle industry in China. *Area Development and Policy*, 4(1), 39–59.

Yu, C. (2016). Bin Li: NIO is a 3.0 company. *Car Consumption Network* (November 14). http://inf.315che.com/n/2016_11/754421/.

Acknowledgments

The first three authors contributed equally to this work. Funding from the Start-up Research Fund of North China University of Technology (grant number: 110051360023XN224-62) made it possible for this Element to be published open access, making the digital version freely available for anyone to read and reuse under a Creative Commons licence.

Cambridge Elements

Business Strategy

J.-C. Spender
Kozminski University

J.-C. Spender is a research Professor, Kozminski University. He has been active in the business strategy field since 1971 and is the author or co-author of 7 books and numerous papers. His principal academic interest is in knowledge-based theories of the private sector firm, and managing them.

Advisory Board

Jay Barney, *Eccles School of Business, The University of Utah*
Stewart Clegg, *University of Technology, Sydney*
Thomas Durand, *Conservatoire National des Arts et Métiers, Paris*
CT Foo, *Independent Scholar, Singapore*
Robert Grant, *Bocconi University, Milan*
Robin Holt, *Copenhagen Business School*
Paula Jarzabkowski, *Cass School, City University, London*
Naga Lakshmi Damaraju, *Indian School of Business*
Marjorie Lyles, *Kelley School of Business, Indiana University*
Joseph T. Mahoney, *College of Business, University of Illinois at Urbana-Champaign*
Nicolai Foss, *Bocconi University, Milan*
Andreas Scherer, *University of Zurich*
Deepak Somaya, *College of Business, University of Illinois at Urbana-Champaign*
Eduard van Gelderen, *Chief Investment Officer, APG, Amsterdam*

About the Series

Business strategy's reach is vast, and important too since wherever there is business activity there is strategizing. As a field, strategy has a long history from medieval and colonial times to today's developed and developing economies. This series offers a place for interesting and illuminating research including industry and corporate studies, strategizing in service industries, the arts, the public sector, and the new forms of Internet-based commerce. It also covers today's expanding gamut of analytic techniques.

Cambridge Elements

Business Strategy

Elements in the Series

People Centric Innovation Ecosystem: Japanese Management and Practices
Yingying Zhang-Zhang and Takeo Kikkawa

Strategizing in the Polish Furniture Industry
Paulina Bednarz-Łuczewska

A Historical Review of Swedish Strategy Research and the Rigor-Relevance Gap
Thomas Kalling and Lars Bengtsson

Global Strategy in Our Age of Chaos: How Will the Multinational Firm Survive?
Stephen Tallman and Mitchell P. Koza

Strategizing With Institutional Theory
Harry Sminia

Effectuation: Rethinking Fundamental Concepts in the Social Sciences
Saras Sarasvathy

Behavioral Strategy: Exploring Microfoundations of Competitive Advantage
Nicolai J. Foss, Ambra Mazzelli and Libby Weber

Digital Assets: A Portfolio Perspective
Henrique Schneider

Diversification in the World of Data and AI
Gianvito Lanzolla and Constantinos Markides

Dynamic Capabilities and Related Paradigms
David J. Teece

Dynamic Capabilities: Foundational Concepts
David J. Teece

The Demise of the Global ICE Industry: China's Stunning Role in Leading the BEV Revolution
Arie Lewin, Martin Kenney, El (Emily) Shu and Liang Mei

A full series listing is available at: www.cambridge.org/EBUS

For EU product safety concerns, contact us at Calle de José Abascal, 56–1°,
28003 Madrid, Spain or eugpsr@cambridge.org.

www.ingramcontent.com/pod-product-compliance
Lightning Source LLC
LaVergne TN
LVHW011856060526
838200LV00054B/4372